SCRIPTURE'S
KNOWING

CASCADE COMPANIONS

The Christian theological tradition provides an embarrassment of riches: from Scripture to modern scholarship, we are blessed with a vast and complex theological inheritance. And yet this feast of traditional riches is too frequently inaccessible to the general reader.

The Cascade Companions series addresses the challenge by publishing books that combine academic rigor with broad appeal and readability. They aim to introduce nonspecialist readers to that vital storehouse of authors, documents, themes, histories, arguments, and movements that comprise this heritage with brief yet compelling volumes.

SCRIPTURE'S KNOWING

A Companion to Biblical Epistemology

DRU JOHNSON

 CASCADE *Books* • Eugene, Oregon

SCRIPTURE'S KNOWING
A Companion to Biblical Epistemology

Cascade Books
An Imprint of Wipf and Stock Publishers
199 W. 8th Ave., Suite 3
Eugene, OR 97401
www.wipfandstock.com

ISBN 13: 978-1-4982-0470-5

Cataloging-in-Publication data:

Johnson, Dru.

Scripture's Knowing : a companion to biblical epistemology.

xxii + 128 p. ; cm. Includes bibliographical references.

ISBN 13: 978-1-4982-0470-5

1. Bible, Epistemology, interpretation, etc. 2. Christian theology. 3. Christian philosophy I. Title.

BT43 J347 2015

Manufactured in the U.S.A.

This companion is dedicated to the all-too-human people who have forced me to think carefully about what the Scriptures say and how that jives with reality. That list spans across my family, my sergeants in the military, my professors, my parishioners, my wife and children, my students, and my current co-laborers in higher education.

It takes a collegial metropolis to raise a junior scholar, and despite my obstinacy, those people tried their hardest with me. So, here's to them for trying!

This book is specifically written for my aunt, Lisa Lancaster, to be read *allegretto*.

CONTENTS

ACKNOWLEDGMENTS

It is difficult to write a book. No one warned me about this before I first tried it.

It is extraordinarily difficult to write a book meant to introduce people to an abstract topic such as epistemology—the theory of knowing. I want to first acknowledge the editorial staff at Cascade Books for encouraging me to tackle this feat. No matter how this particular attempt turns out, they have created a unique publishing platform in the world of theology and biblical studies and fostered junior scholars like me. Further, they have discerned that the rarified air of these academic conversations should be put into the hands of a broader audience in the hopes that something good can happen. Thank you Christian Amondson and everyone at Wipf & Stock for these companions and inviting me to participate!

Beyond Cascade, my doctoral supervisor—Alan Torrance—guided me and opened doors of scholarship for me so that I could stumble around inside. I would be nothing more than a bitter theo-blogging troll in shadows of the Internet—*not that there's anything wrong with that*—without his insights and direction. His oft-quipped saying is right, theology *is* the most fun you can have with your clothes on! The Herzl Institute has been tireless in helping people like me who want to pursue the philosophical structures within Scripture. Yoram Hazony, Josh Weinstein, and Meirav Jones, among others, have been working for years to make a place for this kind of work within Jewish scholarship, and now their labors are pouring into Christian scholars as well. Craig Bartholomew has been a welcoming role model and mentor for me, as well as others associated with the Paideia Centre in Canada and the Scripture and Herme-neutics Seminar. Many of these pages are breathing with the transformational teaching of Esther Meek, to whom I owe so much. Finally, thanks to Ryan O'Dowd for being my remote-colleague in the Ithacan suburbs of New York City. Our regular visits always leave me feeling saner.

A well-regulated dose of thanks goes to Rebecca Au, who cleaned up my textual messes. I am solely to blame for any errors herein. Thanks to those who read drafts of this little book: Shane Krska, Bruno Rocha, and Ken Walker. And finally, without daily care and instruction from my family, I would be hapless and hopeless. I am glad that the kingdom of God shapes me daily through Stephanie, Luisa, Olivia, Claudia, and Benjamin.

INTRODUCTION

Now that I was compelled to think about it, reading was something that just came to me, as learning to fasten the seat of my union suit without looking around, or achieving two bows from a snarl of shoelaces. I could not remember when the lines above Atticus's moving finger separated into words, but I had stared at them all the evenings in my memory . . . Until I feared I would lose it, I never loved to read. One does not love breathing.[1]

—Jean Louise "Scout" Finch

So says Scout Finch, easily recounting the many precious details of her childhood, yet glancing only at the edges of how she actually learned to read. If you did not read the above passage from *To Kill a Mockingbird* (honestly, I would have skipped it too), you should read it closely. I will return to it time and again in the coming chapters.

Reading the words on this page right now, we are all bound up in an act of knowing. Knowing and doing are difficult to separate. Merely thinking about the facts that we know—our wedding anniversary or how many bombs were dropped in Southwest Asia today—we are *doing* something. We can call this *something that we are doing* by different names: thinking, recalling, remembering, cognizing, or

1. Lee, *To Kill a Mockingbird*, 20.

mentally working it out. But whatever we call that act, it seems to be an action that entails a process.

In describing what the Scriptures say, I must also consider that knowing is a process with an outcome. By process, I mean that knowing happens over time and through experiences, which means that our personal history and our bodies are all part of knowing.

Philosophy is the academic discipline traditionally concerned with the processes that produce the most reliable ways of knowing. Logic most often gets thrust forward as the best way to justify our beliefs about the world. Mathematic truths, which are also known through process, help us to feel better about that which we must be sure. For instance, I might not know how many gallons of water fill the ocean. However, I would feel comfortable claiming, "I know that 1+1=2." This mathematic statement seems to be both plainly true and uncontroversial.

For its part, Scripture certainly reasons with the reader using classical logic (e.g., if all wet fleeces amidst dry ground act as a signal from God, then asking for a sign of dry fleece and wet ground acts as confirmation of that divine signal; Judg 6:36–40). Surprisingly, Scripture's process of reasoning does not usually involve things called "beliefs" which we then justify by using a logical calculation. Rather than give facts to plug into logical formulas (e.g., If all men are mortal *and* Socrates is a man, *then* Socrates is mortal), the Hebrew and Christian Scriptures are most often concerned with making Israelites able to see that which is being shown to them. The God of Israel tries to show the pharaoh of Exodus that he and his Egyptian pantheon are not actually in control of fertility, creation, fields, flocks, and more, for instance. By walking Egypt and Israel through that process, Israel's God is trying to show Egypt *and* Israel something which they cannot see unless they submit to the process of knowing. I will discuss this further in Chapter 3.

In *To Kill a Mockingbird*, Scout Finch's insights usually defy her age. However, for those who have spent wearying hours teaching children how to read, fasten buttons, or tie shoelaces, Scout's story of how she magically became a reader is deficient. Like most of us, she does not remember the extended process of learning to read, shot through with:

etiquettes of arrangement (called syntax and grammar),

irregularly spelled strings of symbols (called letters and words),

words of dubious and disparate origins (called "the English language"), and

the rituals of pronunciation that vary by region and class.

Despite her claims about her mysteriously innate ability to read, Scout Finch certainly was put through an extended process meant to help her to cross the threshold—from seeing language as indiscernible jots and squiggles on the page to discernible words and sentences. Once she had crossed that threshold, the words and sentences invariably fade into the background, and now her reading aims onward to meanings and intentions.

BIBLICAL KNOWING

In this book, I want to show that the Christian Scriptures have an interest in portraying a process of knowing that appears to have eluded Scout Finch's memory. Traditionally, the question "How do we know something?" has been consigned to philosophers under a field called "epistemology," from the Greek term meaning to *know how* (literally, to stand over: *epistasthai*). One would presume that Christian philosophers and theologians basically operate with the same view of knowledge (i.e., epistemology) found throughout Christian Scripture. However, I am not sure that this is always, or even often, the case.

As your companion, I would like to divide up this discussion in the coming chapters into more digestible chunks. Biblical scholars, theologians, and Christian philosophers often work unaware of the research done in each others' respective fields. First, I lay out a method for thinking about what a biblical view of knowledge might look like (chapter 1). Second, beginning in the texts of creation, knowing well and avoiding errors is a theme woven into the fabric of the Torah (the Five Books of Moses) and repeated in the gospels (chapters 2–4). Third, the unusual prominence of rituals in biblical knowing deserves special attention (chapter 5). Here, I will discuss how performing a ritual enables knowledge. Fourth, I put my findings from Scripture in conversation with scientific knowing (chapter 6). Surprisingly, we find fortuitous overlap between the two. Fifth, I must answer the "So what?" question (chapter 7). How does this emphasis on knowing affect theology and the life of the church? Finally, I briefly survey some of the work exploring philosophical views of Scripture (chapter 8).

In the end, biblical epistemology appears similar to how scientists come to know, how Scout Finch came to read, and how the disciples came to see what is and is not part of the kingdom of God. Ventures in knowing always require a guide, someone who can authoritatively teach us. Because knowing happens in the social realm, we need reasons to trust our guides. Once they are authenticated to us as trustworthy, our guides direct us to perform actions that will dispose us to see something that we could not see apart from practice: a molecular formation, meaning emerging from words on a page, or a crucifixion as part of God's plan for Jesus to rule his kingdom.

What I propose here cannot be assumed without con-
troversy. Many scholars uncritically assume that the Bible
does not hold clear philosophical positions, much less develop them.[2] This leaves us in the lurch if we want to claim
that "truth" or "knowledge" is a coherent idea throughout
Scripture. If we cannot clarify the biblical position on philosophical ideas, then how can we understand things like
"knowledge" with any confidence?

In attempting to figure out the philosophical ideas of
Scripture, we are doing what is often called "biblical theology," tracing ideas across different books in the Scriptures.
Scholars have debated the usefulness of biblical theology
because most of the authors of Scripture cannot be pinned
down to actual individuals. For example, most scholars
shy away from claiming that Moses wrote Exodus. Hence,
scholars are often unwilling to place the text in a particular
historical setting (e.g., 1250 BCE). For those scholars, it
makes no sense to say that Moses developed a particular
view of knowledge throughout the Torah because those
texts were presumably written by several different groups of
authors and redactors who lived centuries apart from each
other. Moreover, those authors and redactors all employed
different theological and political agendas in their writing.
In light of such a diverse history behind the creation of
these texts, how could such diverse authors have one mind
about topics in metaphysics, ethics, or epistemology?

Regarding differing authors and redactors, an in-
terminable scholarly debate exists in which every side
supposes hypothetical authors of the biblical texts. No
one—orthodox Jews, evangelical Christians, atheist biblical

2. As a quick example, Lynn Rudder Baker evinces this disposition when she says, "The Bible is not a philosophical text; its language
does not point unambiguously to any philosophical position." Baker,
"Christians Should Reject Mind-Body Dualism," 336.

scholars—knows exactly who the biblical authors were with certainty. Scholars become suspicious of hubris when some place too high a degree of confidence in a particular hypothetical author. Hence, I will be sidestepping debates about individual authorship in favor of considering the biblical text in its so-called "final form." Of course, the Hebrew and Christian Scriptures have no absolute final form, but there is a point in Israel's history where a particular set of texts was deemed relevant and revered enough to be put into service as their authoritative Scriptural text, the texts above other texts.[3] Looking across that collection of texts for a discernible pattern of philosophical thinking seems to be a worthwhile effort, even if the authorship varies more (or less even!) than we might have supposed.

THE PROBLEM OF DISCERNING PHILOSOPHY IN THE BIBLE

To the matter of unclear philosophical positions in Scripture, reading the Bible as literature can help to clarify some basic presumptions. For instance, considering the narrative structure of a passage can often help us to understand why the author included certain narrative details and excluded others. In the attempted sacrifice of Isaac (Gen 22), the structure of the story itself indicates that the story's resolution centers upon YHWH and Abraham coming to specific sorts of knowledge. YHWH now knows that Abraham fears him (i.e., Gen 22:12). Abraham and Isaac now know that YHWH has provided (i.e., Gen 22:14).

---

3. Though genuinely impossible to get scholars to agree on what that collection of texts is, we can take the most primitive collection that appears to coincide with the Masoretic Texts in the *Biblia Hebraica Stuttgartensia* and the eclectic texts in Nestle-Aland's New Testament, 28th ed.

Scholars have examined every detail in that short story for a reason—to explain what appears to us as God's immoral request. Or, they've turned over the story to attempt to reconstruct whether or not Abraham should have told YHWH "no!" when YHWH puts him to the test. No shortage of motivation exists for theologians to find an ethical theory that would spare us moderns from attempting to kill our children if we were convinced that God told us to. However, the structure of the narrative itself points the listening ear to the climax and resolution of the story, which is followed by an emphatic doubling of the story's concluding remark: "So Abraham called the name of that place 'YHWH provides,' as it is said to this day: 'On the mount of YHWH it shall be provided'" (Gen 22:14).[4] Abraham's focus on provision rises above other matters glaring at us from the narrative. However, the structure of the story itself signals that the narrator shows little interest in our most pressing question: what kind of a god would ask a man to kill his son—his only son—whom he loves? Further, doggedly pursuing our own pressing question with the goal of reconciling it to an ethical theory might distort our ability to hear why the author tells *this* story with *these* details.

Giving the author the privilege of telling the story means that we allow the narrator to put us in a process by which we come to see what the narrator is showing us. Is the narrative trying to show us the inner-moral reason of Abraham's God here, or the responsive trust of Abraham in YHWH's provision? I would argue for the latter, but whatever we think it might be, we should let the narrator have the privilege of showing us. Only after this process of coming to know can we then revisit the text with more questions. As Esther Meek contends in her book *Longing to Know*, when

4. "YHWH provides" could also be translated "YHWH sees," as in "YHWH sees to it."

we come to know, our questions are not answered, they are transformed into new and better questions.[5]

In our first reading of a text, I want to give priority to the story's structure over and above our questions, which must be answered, modified, or dismissed in their turn. This disciplined reading will yield fruits that can serve our theology. Of course, all theologies will inform our readings, for better or worse, but we should avoid letting our theology predetermine our reading of the biblical texts—shielding us from the disruptive influence of Scripture on our clean and constructed theological categories.

Which texts should we consider for examination? I am using three criteria to decide which texts and passages merit in-depth consideration for the biblical thinking on epistemology: *presence*, *relevance*, and *persistence*. The criterion of *presence* means a passage has a demonstrated pattern of language associated with knowing, even when terms such as "know," "believe," and "truth" do not show up in that text. Although the Hebrew and Greek terms for "know" and "knowledge" occur quite frequently throughout Scripture, the terms alone are not sufficient to denote a passage worth pursuing. In fact, some of the most epistemologically significant passages will barely mention "knowledge," but contain other terms that signal an important description of knowledge. For instance, biblical authors most often employ the term "seeing" to act as the primary metaphor for knowing, much the same way we use it in English today: "Oh, I see!" (Do you see what I did there?) Hence, we cannot simply search for the term "know" throughout the Bible and suppose that we have somehow wrangled biblical accounts of knowing into our corral.

Beyond the mere *presence* of key terms, "knowing" must be *relevant* to the text under consideration. For

5. Meek, *Longing to Know*, 79–80.

example, Genesis 4 contains three instances of the Hebrew term "know" (*yada*), all of which are meant to describe successful procreation between spouses. The presence of "know" in those passages means "to have sex with" in our English vernacular. I do not consider it an accident that "knowing" and "sexual intimacy" are easily related to each other in the Hebrew. Nevertheless, the sex embedded into the Cain and Abel story (Gen 4:1, 17, 25) is not directly *relevant* to acts of knowing writ large—at least, not without a robust exploration of knowledge already developed from somewhere beyond Genesis 4.

Presuming that we have a passage where knowing is both *present* and *relevant* to the author's task (so far as can be discerned), we do not yet have a candidate for a biblical account of knowing. The final criterion—*persistence*—asks whether or not this is a one-off depiction of knowledge. If so, then we should remain skeptical as to its helpfulness in building a case for biblical knowing. Basically, the author of a particular book must have a demonstrable interest in developing a view of knowing through *persistent* use of stories where knowing is *relevant*. One easy example of this *persistence*, among many, is the book of Exodus. In Exodus 1–14, well over a dozen instances of "you will know" occur in relation to YHWH performing signs and wonders in Egypt. The passage through the Red Sea then poetically calls Israel to "see" this wonder as the hand of YHWH. This "seeing" most basically demands that they understand that YHWH's power afforded their miraculous escape (i.e., not the power of the Egyptian gods). Then, as the Israelites wander initially in need of water and food, manna is sent specifically for the purpose of knowing that "I am YHWH your God" (Exod 16:12). After some legal instruction, the first problem that develops in Exodus 32 centers upon Israel's misunderstanding about who brought her out of Egypt.

Appallingly, the Israelites cry out concerning the golden calf that Aaron has carved: "These are your gods [presumably the golden calf and YHWH], O Israel, who brought you out of the land of Egypt" (Exod 32:4). Knowledge is clearly *present*, directly *relevant* to the unfolding history of Israel, and *persistently* developed throughout the narrative portion of Exodus.

My intention here is to pursue those things clearly highlighted by their prominent position and repetition in the Bible—what Jaco Gericke calls the biblical authors' "folk philosophical beliefs."[6] With this methodology and careful consideration of similar patterns across the Scriptures, I hope to show the basic merits in pursuing a philosophically sensitive biblical theology.

A NOTE ON BIBLICAL PASSAGES

In the coming chapters, I will examine three foundational areas of Scripture: the creation narratives, the exodus, and the gospels.[7] The reason for this stems from my own conviction that these texts are foundational. By that, I mean that in order to read all other parts of Scripture—the conquest of Canaan, the kingdoms of Israel, the prophets, the exile and return, the epistles of Paul, or Revelation—a prior understanding of the creation narratives, the Torah more generally, and the gospels is requisite. Conversely, failure to understand the Torah produces an impoverished understanding of other biblical texts while the opposite is not

6. Gericke, *Hebrew Bible and Philosophy of Religion*, 206.

7. Because this is part of the *Cascade Companion* series, and because it relies heavily on biblical exegesis, a more detailed account of the exegesis behind these claims is offered in *Biblical Knowing*. If one wants even more detail of the exegesis, see Andrew M. Johnson, "Error and Epistemological Process"; Dru Johnson, *Biblical Theology and Epistemology*.

necessarily true. I hope to show why this is the case in the coming chapters.

Nota Bene: I will be using the noun "epistemology" and the adjective "epistemological" in the coming chapters so please begin to feel comfortable with the term. Many people, even scholars, glaze over when they hear these terms, so I will try to use them sparingly. To be clear, when I say "epistemological," I basically mean, "has to do with knowing." It's just easier to use one word than coming up with variations of "has to do with knowing."

Unless otherwise stated, translations of the biblical texts are my own.

1

KNOWING

Biblical Language and Concepts

"Illumination"...is the plunge by which we gain a foothold at another shore of reality.

Michael Polanyi[1]

I WILL NEED THE reader to bear with me for a few paragraphs.

Michael Polanyi portrays the moment of scientific discovery—what he calls "illumination"—as crossing a lake, landing on a far shore with a new vista of reality. Similarly, philosopher Esther Meek begins her definition of "knowing" by framing it as an act: "Knowing is the responsible human struggle."[2] Struggles happen over time and through the human body. Struggles are *responsible* only when we struggle for a purpose. Meek claims that as humans, we are not gifted with instantaneous knowledge. Rather, we must work for it. As all parents know, even grasping that "1+1=2" requires some initial effort to understand—even if the likes of Scout Finch no longer recall *the struggle*. I bring up basic

1. Polanyi, *Personal Knowledge*, 123.
2. Meek, *Longing to Know*, 53.

addition here because most philosophers will go to mathematic examples when attempting to demonstrate their ideas about knowledge. Biblical authors, however, will not appeal to mathematics as examples to examine knowledge, though I believe they have something similar in mind.

When we use math as a proof of knowledge today, we are using the ideas associated with rigor and clarity in our culture. For us, one plus one *just is* two, and our access to its truth appears to us as universal—anyone can *just see* that it's true. Scientist-turned-philosopher Michael Polanyi argues that an "illumination," the "aha moment" of discovery, isn't just a moment. That moment *just is* the culmination of the struggle to know. If even math requires striving and effort in order to understand the basics of addition, then we ought to think about what math proves and how it does so before we look at the Scriptures for a model of good knowing.

As an example, if two oranges and one apple lay on the table, a person with the basic skills of counting will have to observe what is on the table to determine that there are three pieces of fruit. Knowing that two oranges plus one apple makes three fruits reveals a learned and skilled process (e.g., discerning fruits from other objects). In order for humans to have that skill to *just see* that there are three pieces of fruit on the table, they must struggle to acquire the skill.

Even the ability to count objects (i.e., one orange, two oranges, three oranges, etc.) must be taught through rituals of repetition so that our ability to number objects comes through processes that we learned with our bodies as children. In a cruel twist of humanity, most of the work in teaching children these frustratingly simple skills is done in the period of their life that they simply will not remember.

Benjamint444, *Navel orange1;* **Mgmoscatello,** *Apple picture.*

As these skills are built up in us through those formative years, we are able to use them more quickly to solve simple problems, problems that were previously insurmountable to us before learning the skill. If asked how many pieces of fruit were on the table, I can easily assert "three" just by glancing. If pressed about how I came to the answer, I might report, "I *just saw* that there were three." If asked when I learned to make such quick accountings, like Scout Finch I could naively say, "I've just always known how." Without any parents or teachers to disabuse me of my ignorance, I could get away with such a belief about my counting ability.

Why am I talking about basic math in a chapter about biblical views of knowing? Because even when I have the ability to *just see* something, and even when it's a genuine ability, that skill extends from a history of practicing, guided by adults, in order that I might be able to *just see* that $2+1=3$. Anecdotally, parents can become frustrated with their child's math homework because the parent does not understand how the child cannot *just see* the plain mathematic truth of "$2+1=3$." As children, we struggled *responsibly* to see what is plain and obvious to adults. In short, knowing—even knowing basic math—is a *process*, and the moment of discovery is an *event*.

Examining the event without the process can create problematic views of knowledge. Problematic because they have little regard for the human body, community, and process in which they are bound up. For those interested in the biblical discourse, the ancient authors of Scripture regularly maintain the connection of the embodied person in her community struggling to understand reality over the course of time.

Knowing appears to be an acquired skill per the biblical authors. A skill is practiced until we achieve the knack for it, such as riding a bike or reading an X-ray. A child *with the skill* can just hop on a bike and go. A doctor who *has the knack* can *just see* a tumor in an X-ray film. However, the biblical authors presume that you must gain the skill through a guided process in order to see. Like a parent coaching their child's first ride without training wheels or a medical student in a radiology course, we must embody guided processes in order to know. Once skilled, you see the world differently. Knowing is transformative, what Polanyi depicts as "the plunge by which we gain a foothold at another shore of reality."[3] Because it's a skill, once you have it, the skill transforms you to *just see* something you could not previously see. You are different and, therefore, see differently.

If the biblical authors do not use mathematical examples to examine a theory of knowledge, then what is their version of rigor and clarity? Thinking through some examples might help, though they may not look very mathematical to us at first. In Genesis 3, the man and the woman of Eden *just see* that they are naked and hide themselves accordingly (Gen 3:7). In Exodus, the Israelites *just see* that YHWH[4] opened the Red Sea and destroyed Pharaoh's army (Exod 14:30–31). Conversely, the disciples do not see what Jesus is up to in Mark's gospel (cf. Mark 8:17–18; 31–33). In Luke's gospel, the disciples cannot even see that the resurrected Jesus is, in fact, the man walking with them for miles (Luke 24:31). I will return to show how these passages rigorously examine good knowing in the coming chapters.

---

3. Polanyi, *Personal Knowledge*, 123.

4. "YHWH" or "Yahweh" is the Hebrew four-lettered name often translated "the LORD" in modern English Bibles for reasons of tradition. I will use YHWH to refer to the God of Israel who variously is called "God" (*El* or *Elohim*), the LORD (*YHWH*), and Lord (*Adonai*) throughout the Hebrew Bible.

In each case, the reader is presented with facts of the matter that the story's logic considers plain and clear—as plain as "1+1=2." The nakedness of the first couple, the work of YHWH against Egypt, that Jesus is the prophet of Israel, and that it was Jesus himself walking along with disciples to Emmaus are as plain to the reader as basic math. Indeed, they are painfully obvious to us readers.

What enables the characters in these stories to *just see* these plain facts or be entirely blind to them? In other words, what establishes a clear difference between those who can see and those who cannot? Amazingly, the biblical texts *are* interested in examining such questions. These Scriptures, written and collected over the centuries, have an interest in developing a philosophical position on knowing:

1. what the process of knowing requires,

2. how one becomes a better knower,

3. and crucially, how one can avoid erroneous knowing.

In fact, the biblical texts show a high interest in clarifying what good knowing consists of. The Hebrew Bible opens with a creation story that centers upon knowing good and evil (Gen 2:17), knowing nakedness (Gen 3:7), and then sexual knowing (Gen 4:1). Hence, knowing is not a side-show to the biblical narratives, but front and center in the story of Israel.

LANGUAGE ABOUT KNOWING IN SCRIPTURE

Before looking at those ancient Semitic texts, we must consider how we might import foreign ideas into the discussion, mostly due to the translation of terms. Grappling with the distance between our connotations in English and the use of "knowing" language in the Scriptures helps us become better readers. It's as if we are packing for a trip to Thailand, when our flight is actually headed to Siberia. We have some things that will still work (e.g., pants, shoes, camera, etc.), but we are woefully underprepared to survive in that Siberian world. Likewise, if we come to the biblical texts presuming that knowledge is something akin to "data" or "information," then we might be woefully unprepared to see what the biblical authors are attempting to show us.

Hence, I mostly avoid using the noun "knowledge." In the world of my undergraduate students, knowledge is most often conceived of as an object, a thing to possess. The queerness of modern English does not help to clarify the matter. In English, for instance, we say that we *have* knowledge. We *have* sex. But in what way do we *have* either of them? My students often want to "get" knowledge and they wrongly assume that I am there as the professor to "give" it to them. Indeed, many false expectations of college courses stem from their wrong notions of education as an exchange of commodities.

Rather, most educators (and on a good day, that includes professors) see a college course as a series of embodied historical practices that are meant to change the way students see the object of study. I regularly teach an introduction to the Hebrew Bible (Old Testament) and my main goal is for them to read the actual texts and see things they have never noticed before—to have a skilled reading acquired through discipline and practice. Hence, knowing functions as a way of seeing the same "data," but with skilled eyes—like a doctor sees a tumor in an X-ray that is indiscernible to you or me.

To know is to act with skill, and so discussing knowing in terms of "knowledge," "data," or "information" can detract from our understanding, even if we grasp what nouns such as "data" are meant to convey. To salaciously illustrate the point, what could it mean if someone asked: Do you *have* carnal knowledge of your spouse? What one knows, in response to this question, is not possession of information about another person. In other words, one spouse does not *have* anything when it comes to sexual knowledge. There is no room for the answer to consist of "data." Fortunately, the analogy breaks down quickly from there, so I need not pursue it any further.

In the Scriptures, we should not expect that those authors frame knowing as data to be possessed, *and this does not make their view of knowledge antiquated or irrelevant.* Unhelpfully, the key terms from Hebrew and Greek have been translated in ways that do not always reveal their native meaning to the modern ear. Without getting into the dizzying array of meanings that words can take, we ought to consider how the basic biblical language and the concepts associated with knowing line up with our language and concepts.

True/Truth

Modern folk are comfortable talking about "the truth" as if it is a thing. We know *the truth* or not. *The fact* is either true or false. Some people can't handle *the truth. The truth* will set you free (unless you are actually guilty).

Truth has become an object in our thinking, something to have and to hold. However, the Hebrew word group most often translated as "true" relates to a specific aspect of truth in English: fidelity. In fact, one of the few Hebrew words to sneak into the English language occurs at the end of our affirmation of a faithful petition to God. We close prayer by affirming: Amen. Amen comes from the Hebrew *aman*, which is the root word for several terms related to accuracy, fidelity, and faithfulness. When the North African Jewish community translated the Hebrew Bible into

Greek, they chose a particular Greek term to translate the Hebrew "truth" (*emet*): *aletheia*. As it so happens, *aletheia* also carries the connotations of fidelity and faithfulness in the Greek.

So it should not surprise us that the meaning of "true," as used in the Scriptures, mostly relates to the reliability of something to support, to be faithful, to be steady, to have high fidelity, and therefore *something in which we can put our trust*. True can describe the fidelity of a boat's path to a course set in advance, or of a carpenter's cut to a line drawn on lumber. Because "true" (*aman*) is an adjective throughout the Hebrew Bible, it can be readily conceptualized as a noun: truth (*emet*). Even the New Testament authors felt free to conceptualize truth as a noun: Jesus is the way, the truth (*aletheia*), and the life (John 14:6).

As an adjective, "true" describes a surprising array of objects and actions in the Hebrew Bible, all of which are related directly to fidelity and faithfulness. Actions can be true.[5] Reports and statements can reliably convey the situation.[6] Most strangely, many biblical authors use "true" to describe objects such as tent pegs (Isa 22:23), roads (Gen 24:38), seeds (Jer 2:21), and more.

How is a tent peg true in the same way that reports or actions are true? Yoram Hazony explores this oddity in *The Philosophy of Hebrew Scripture*, and I follow him closely here. Hazony consistently points out that truth is not something that can be assessed in a moment, but a quality that is borne out over "time and circumstance."

> What we really hope for when we drive this
> peg into the ground is something normative:
> We want it to be what a tent-peg *ought to be* (in

5. E.g., treatment toward a servant (Gen 32:11), anointing (Judg 9:15), walking (1 Kgs 2:4), etc.

6. E.g., Deut 13:14; 17:4.

our estimation) in the face of the stresses and strains of the storm.

In the Hebrew Bible, that which is true is that which proves, in the face of time and circumstance, to be what it ought; whereas that which is false is that which fails . . . to be what it ought.[7]

This means that the biblical notion of knowing truth and knowing it truly must regard the priority of skillfully seeing something to be true "in the face of time and circumstance."

The picture does not change radically in the New Testament, where truth (*aletheia*) describes people,[8] actions,[9] statements,[10] realizations,[11] and becomes a metaphor for the faithful instruction of God: "the truth" (e.g., Rom 1:25; 2:8). In fact, truthfulness becomes a supreme quality of important statements according to Jesus himself: "Truly (*alethos*) I say to you," describing his speech as aptly guiding his followers, not merely as statements of truth (Luke 12:44).

In short, truth is personal in the biblical texts. It requires *our* attention and *our* expectations over time. When something is true, it does what it ought to do or faithfully represents—it is trustworthy. This creates a very natural segue to a similar word group: trust.

7. Hazony, *Philosophy of Hebrew Scripture*, 201.

8. E.g., Jesus, Matt 22:16; teacher, Mark 12:14; worshipers, John 4:23.

9. E.g., practicing truth, John 3:21; standing in truth, 8:44; sanctifying in truth, 17:17.

10. Mark 5:53; Luke 4:25; Acts 26:25.

11. Matt 27:54; Mark 14:17.

Believe/Trust/Faith

What does it mean to "have faith"? When I asked this question in a public university classroom, the most common response was, "To believe without reasons or evidence." Some students were then surprised at the genuine difficulty in naming one instance in the Christian Scriptures where someone "has faith" without any reason, deliberation, or evidence. I challenge my classes every semester to show me anywhere in Scripture where YHWH asks someone to trust him without any prior reasons given. There might be a few places—but literally, only a few. The term for "believe" or "trust" (sometimes translated "faith") in the Hebrew Bible comes from the same word group above: *aman*. Though from the same basic word, the form of the word and context allow it to mean "to trust" or "to believe." The Septuagint—the Greek translation of the Hebrew Bible—recognizes that difference by translating those Hebrew words with a different word: *pisteuo*, which more exclusively relates to trust and/or belief in the Greek.

It appears to me as irresponsible to translate a word that basically relates the idea of trust with the English term "faith," a word that almost universally connotes blind obedience to the modern ear. Even translating it as "believe" makes beliefs appear as something more in a mental sphere than the embodied actions of the biblical protagonists. In modern English, "to believe" can even mean "to have an opinion about." In most instances throughout Scripture, the translated words "faith" and "belief/believe" could be replaced with "trust" or "trusting belief" for truer resemblance to the biblical vocabulary.

Moreover, the translation of *aman/pisteuo* into the English word "trust" has another advantage: it forces us to look for the object or person to be trusted. For example, when Jesus appears resurrected to all but one disciple

(Thomas), the other disciples who saw him tell Thomas about what they had seen. Thomas insists that unless he himself touches the resurrected Jesus, he will "never believe (*pisteuso*)" (John 20:25). So, Jesus appears expressly for the purpose of allowing Thomas to touch his wounds—charging Thomas, "Do not disbelieve, but believe" (John 20:27). Jesus goes on to bless those who do not see, but believe (John 20:29). And then the gospel narrator sums up the book with "these are written so that you [the reader or hearer] may believe" (John 20:31). We could even change all the language to be in terms of "having faith." Notice what the language of "believe" and "have faith" does *not* do to the modern reader. *It does not force us to ask the most natural question*: Have faith (or believe) *in what* or *whom*? If we translate all the same terms to "trust," the story becomes a bit more forceful with us as readers. Let me retell it briefly this way:

The disciples, sans Thomas, see Jesus.

The disciples report it to Thomas.

Thomas says, "Unless I touch him, I will never trust."

Jesus appears and says, "Touch my wounds. Be not untrusting, but trusting."

John's narrator sums up, "These were written so that you may trust."

Trust who? The conflict in this narrative centers upon Thomas not trusting the testimony of the disciples who saw Jesus. Jesus shows up to prove the disciples' testimony as *true*—faithful to reality and doing what it ought to do. The narrator interjects that this entire literary creation—the Gospel of John—was aimed at fostering trust in the disciples' testimony, which is what the gospel is meant to represent: the true testimony of the disciple John. Translating this term as "trust" forces us to ask different questions.

Merely depicting Jesus as commending Thomas to "have faith" obscures the force of the story.

Like sex, faith is not an object to have. Faith is always *faith in* something. As Andrew Walker and Robin Parry recently put it: "Faith in Jesus is, first and foremost, an existential commitment to and trust in Jesus; 'belief *in* . . .' and not simply 'belief *that*.'"[12] Our best term in English for translating what is most often meant by *aman* in the Hebrew Bible and *pisteuo* in the Greek is "trust," not "belief" or "faith."

Know/Sexually Join

Unless you live in a cultural cave, you already have some contact with the Hebrew word for "know." He is small, green, quick on his aged feet, and English syntax not good with he is. "Yoda" is Hebrew for "knower," or, "one who knows."

In Hebrew, "to know" (*yada*) has a surprising range of meaning. The term can refer to someone's familiarity, understanding, historical recall, skilled insight, and most striking, sexual intimacy. "To know," just within the first four chapters of Genesis, includes the ever-ambiguous knowledge of good and evil, knowledge of nakedness, and three instances of successful procreation (cf. Gen 2:17; 3:6; 4:1, 17, 25; 19:5). Because of this range of meaning, Michael Carasik and Gerhard von Rad offer the simplest view, that "to know" connoted the idea of "coming closer to" for the ancient Israelite.[13] The sexual connotation of "know" (*yada*), "is right in so far as the verb *yd'* ('to know') never signifies purely intellectual knowing, but rather an 'experiencing,' a

---

12. Walker and Parry, *Deep Church Rising*, 70.

13. Carasik, *Theologies of the Mind*, 20.

'becoming acquainted with.'"[14] As we consider the sensory language in the Bible that depicts good knowing ("listen" and "see"), it will become obvious that a biblical view of knowing always entails the individual's body, the social body (i.e., *the body politic*), time, and a distinct process that must be acted out.

In the Greek, there are two verbs associated with knowing: *ginosko* (noun: *gnosis*) and *oida*. The first is where we get the English terms "*gnostic*" or "dia*gnosis*." It generally refers to the same range of meanings as the Hebrew term *yada*. The second literally means "to see" (*oida*) and is used to convey understanding or insight. *Ginosko* can include meanings such as "skill" or "familiarity," which might be why it is the verb that also translates sexual union in the Septuagint (i.e., "Adam *knew* his wife"; Gen 4:1).

Surprisingly, in the gospel narratives, these Greek words for "know" are less important than their reliance upon the Septuagint,[15] which contains its own compelling view of knowledge. As I said in the Introduction, it will not always be the case that the word "know" even has to appear in a text in order for it to be concerned with epistemology. For instance, Mark's gospel borrows heavily from the language and concepts of Deuteronomy and Isaiah to convey when someone knows well or erroneously. Mark's language rarely involves the Greek terms *oida* or *ginosko*. Instead, Mark relies on a well known and patterned use of *listening in order to see* that he appears to borrow from Deuteronomy and Isaiah. We will look at Deuteronomy, Isaiah, and Mark in chapter 4. For now, we briefly turn our attention to those epistemic terms—listen and see.

14. Rad, *Genesis*, 79.

15. The Septuagint (abbrev. LXX) is the Greek translation of the Hebrew Bible in common use during the intertestamental period of Hellenistic Judaism.

Listen/See

Just as in modern English, the Scriptures rely heavily on sensory terms for descriptions of knowing. For instance, these are some ways—colloquial and not—we still talk about knowing with some of our sensory language.

Touch: to grasp; to get it; to latch onto; to take it in; to apprehend; etc.

Sight: to have an in*sight*; to foresee; "Do you see what I'm saying?"; to get the picture; to read her like a book, etc.

We even use "taste" to convey our knowledge of something (e.g., the taste of defeat) and discriminating judgment (e.g., Her condo was decorated with taste.). Smell can reflect intuitiveness (e.g., Something doesn't smell right about this.). And, hearing has a wide range of associations with our discernment and knowing in English. We speak of knowing as being informed: "Did you hear about the invasion?" Court cases are conceptualized as *a hearing*: "The judge heard the case." We affirm our acknowledgment with our ears: "I hear what you're saying."

Although sensory terms have some similar uses in the biblical languages, two verbs clearly rise to prominence as indicators of knowing: "listen" and "see."[16] It also happens to be the case in both Hebrew and Greek that there are not separate words to mean "listen" and "obey." So in many cases, we will see that "listening to his voice" actually means, "obeying."

The grammatical form of the word and its context determines which English term ends up in the translation. "To see" takes on most of the varied uses we have in English. "To see" (Hebrew: *ra'ah*; Greek: *horao*) can mean visually witnessing, to "get it," to be aware, to understand, or to know. Most basically, understanding how these two terms—listen

16. Avrahami, *The Senses of Scripture*, 69–74.

and see—take a particular order in biblical knowing will have remarkable implications throughout all of Scripture.

The basic structure is this: *In order to know well, you must listen to trusted authorities and do what they say in order to see what they are showing you.* That's it. The varied literary style of biblical authors certainly defies attempts to make this language formulaic. Different books have different ways of expressing this simple epistemological conviction. However, the stock use of this language is sufficient enough for us to trace it throughout the Torah (the books of Moses) and into the gospels.

Though "listen and see" could simply mean "pay attention," there is a priority to them because, again, listening also connotes obedience (Hebrew: *shama*; Greek: *akouo*). Listening, or heeding, the trusted authority must come first. The authority knows what must be done in order to see what is being shown. Hence, listening to her voice means doing what she says. It makes no sense to act and then get instruction. That would be like assembling a complicated piece of Swedish flat-pack furniture, and only afterward, looking at the directions. Presumably, loose parts will be strewn about afterward.

GOING FORWARD

Two matters concern us in the coming chapters. First, what is this biblical view of knowing and how can we discern it? Again, in the most plain terms possible: *Knowing well entails listening to trusted authorities and doing what they prescribe in order to see what they are showing you.* That is the central idea. Therefore, the coming chapter will test the idea. If correct, then we should expect to find an emphasis on listening to the trusted authority, and then embodying her instruction, with the outcome of knowing something—seeing something not previously noticed or truly seeing the same data (i.e., the correct way).

Second, is this a view of religious knowledge? I will later show that this social process of knowing described in the biblical literature lays out the foundational ideas that scientific inquiry follows today. In reality, the only thing that separates good biblical knowing from good scientific knowing is the way in which trusted authorities gain our trust. In the end, "science" is most aptly described as a community of knowers who must trust each other while soberly observing some specific facet of reality. In order to become a good scientist, you must trust authoritative guides (e.g., biology professors) who will prescribe rituals to be embodied (e.g., preparing slides for a microscope) in order to see what is being shown (e.g., cell wall deterioration). Failure to recognize who should be trusted or heed the authority's instruction results in erroneous knowing or accidental knowing, neither of which are desirable.

In the coming chapters, I will demonstrate both that the biblical literature pursues the idea of a knowing well in community and that we can see that creational function at work in places like the scientific enterprise today.

FOR DISCUSSION

1. What are some basic facts that Christians often cite as "the truth"?

2. Name some facts that you *just see* to be true? What processes led you to the point where you could *just see* those things as plainly true?

3. How important is the language we use to communicate biblical ideas (e.g., truth, certainty, doubt, faith, etc.)?

2

KNOWING IN THE CREATION

Voices Carry

AMONG THE DIVERSE BIBLICAL texts, some portions set the theological stage for the rest. In other words, some stories in Scripture take priority. For instance, I have argued elsewhere that the creation narrative, the exodus from Egypt, and the Gospels play a prominent role in how we read the rest of Scripture.[1] For the sake of efficiency, I will only focus on four key stories in the coming chapters: Eden (Gen 2–3), the exodus (Exod 1–14), disciple-making (Mark 4–9), and knowing the resurrected Jesus (Luke 24).

If the central idea about knowing is correct, then we should expect to see an emphasis on establishing trusted authorities whom the Israelites should heed. In order to know, heeding means that they embody the instructions being prescribed. Sometimes, aspects of good knowing

1. Dru Johnson, *Biblical Knowing*, xv–xxi. One could argue that the exile shares such prominence in the theology of Israel; although, I would argue that the exile is conceptually present in the creation narrative (Gen 3:23–24) and much of the Torah, especially Deuteronomy (Deut 28–30).

18

surface only after proper knowing has broken down. Like an engineer who comes to know the hairline fracturing of a steel beam only after it snaps under pressure, biblical narratives often highlight how *not* to know as much as how to know properly. Putting these stories together, we will see both the proper means of knowing and specific procedural violations to be avoided.

In this chapter, I want to show how Genesis 2 and 3 operate as two distinct pictures of knowing: knowing that goes well and knowing that goes awry. In both cases, a person is led by an authority who guides them to see what is being shown to them. Both stories are epistemological and resolve with an epiphany—seeing that the woman is man's fit mate and the couple knowing they are shamefully naked. In both cases, an authority is heeded, a prescribed process is performed, and knowing is the natural outcome.

If you do not have all the details of Genesis 2–3 memorized, then you should stop here, take a minute, and read those two chapters closely, especially Genesis 2:15—3:19. These well-known stories are often studied for their climactic and theological features, but less often so for their literary features. Indeed, if you think of Genesis 3 as "The Fall" or a story of moral autonomy, then you will need to reread with me. I suggest that an equally apt term to describe this pair of stories is "The Shift."

I begin in Genesis 2 because it's a story explicitly about knowing. The man is formed, given the "breath of life," put into the garden to work and keep it, and commanded, "Eating, you will eat from every tree of the garden" (Gen 2:16). Notably, the man receives this command before the woman is constructed from his bone and flesh. There is also a condition added to the man's vocation: "But, from the tree of knowledge of good and evil you shall not eat from it, for in the day you eat from it, dying, you will die" (Gen 2:17).

The entire story of Genesis 3 turns on the matter of knowing: *who* knows *what* and *how*. The man and woman later *know* that they are naked, something already known to the reader, through the prescribed act of eating. In the very first story of human interaction, we have persons in community, listening to an authority, heeding his words, performing his prescribed actions, and then coming to know their nakedness—a thoroughly embodied and social view of knowledge. So what is the problem? They trust the serpent and enact his instruction.

I want to make two broad observations from this inaugural storyline. First, there is a proper act of knowing prior to the serpent's entry into the garden. Second, though myriad authors have tackled this story for all kinds of reasons, YHWH's diagnosis of the problem in Genesis 3 often goes without comment in most treatments of the Eden story. This extraordinary omission hinders us from considering key aspects to the story.

GENESIS 2

> This is, at last, bone from my bone and flesh from my flesh. This I will call woman, from man this was taken. (Gen 2:23)

How is this a story about knowing? In short, the man comes to know that the woman resolves the problem of his aloneness. Apart from the intimation of sexual knowledge in the seven-day creation account (Gen 1:28), the man's discovery that the woman is his fit mate offers the first glimpse into a canonical view of knowledge. The elements of knowing are all here. The narrative's conflict begins by YHWH's assessment, "It is not good for the man to be alone. I will fashion for him a helper corresponding to him" (Gen 2:18).

Thus, YHWH knows that man should not be alone and that YHWH will make a suitable helpmate. Does the man know this?

Though not patently obvious in the story, I want to suggest that through heeding the guidance of YHWH, the man comes to know who is his fit mate (i.e., the woman) and who is not (i.e., all the other animals that he named). Obviously, Genesis 2:18–20 does not say the man follows instructions in order to know. Rather, it does portray YHWH as the lead actor, presenting various creatures to the man for him to name with the result that, "for the man, he did not find for himself a fit helper" (Gen 2:20).[2] YHWH leads him to know what his fit mate is not, and we soon find out that his discovery emphasizes this contrast. It's as if he has been primed to recognize his proper mate by reviewing all the creatures that she is not. It is akin to trying a ring full of keys on a lock, knowing which keys are wrong before knowing which is correct.[3]

In this story, the priming works. After the man sees the woman *constructed* from his bone and flesh, her similitude allows him to know that she is the resolution to his aloneness. He exclaims, "At last (*hapa'am*), bone of my bone and flesh of my flesh," also calling her "woman" because she was literally "taken from man" (Hebrew: *ishah* because she was taken from *ish*; Gen 2:23).

2. Cassuto effectively argues that "to find" should be translated as the reflexive, "he did not find for himself," rather than, "was not found for him." In other words, the man is doing the finding and no one else. Cassuto, *Commentary on the Book of Genesis*, 133.

3. This analogy works, as long as we do not take Rabbi Eliezar's suggestions from the Talmud too seriously: "This teaches that Adam had intercourse with every beast and animal but found no satisfaction until he cohabited with Eve." Babylonian Talmud: Tractate Yevamoth 63a.

What cannot be missed is that the man comes to know his proper mate through a process of naming, not discovering a fit mate, and then recognizing what was taken out and constructed from him. So Karl Barth says of this passage: "The whole story aims at this exclamation [At last!]."[4]

This gets to an ancient philosophical quandary: How can we know that which we do not know? In order to recognize something, it seems like we must have had some prior familiarity with it. Plato resolves this problem by affirming exactly that. Through the voice of Socrates, he claims that we have all had knowledge of the perfect eternal forms of chairs, horses, houses, etc. in the heavenlies prior to being incarnated.[5] We recognize the horse-ness of the horse, because of our pre-incarnate experience with its perfect and unchanging horse-form in the heavens.

On the contrary, the Genesis story requires no previous knowledge or familiarity. The man comes to know from an historical process of naming guided by YHWH. Two facets appear to shape his process of discovery: (1) YHWH primes the man to discover by naming unfit mates and (2) the man understands that a suitable helpmate entails that his mate must be fundamentally similar to himself. To be cliché: he came to know that they were made for each other.

Because the goal of knowing here appears to be functional/relational knowledge, not objective and static data, his discovery can make sense to us. The first time I laid cinderblock, I could not have told you what was the best tool to complete that task. However, after using several of the wrong tools, I could not find for myself a fit instrument. Only after someone presented me with a masonry trowel could I exclaim: At last, a tool that does the job most

4. Barth, *Church Dogmatics*, 291.

5. Plato's discussion of the forms can be found in the *Meno*.

suitably! Such discoveries seem plausible if they consist of embodied understanding of how something functions.

It is no surprise that we have long been interested in figuring out objective knowledge, that which can be known independent of a particular time or circumstance. Our desire to examine knowledge, time, space, being, relations, and ethics *as such*, has taken philosophers down a path to free their inquiries of subjective premises and the restrictions of local functional knowledge. The goal of this pursuit was to arrive at a core set of fundamental truths, not subject to "time and circumstance." It's fair to say that philosophy has now given up on that quest as a totalizing view of knowledge, though remnants of it persist in some quarters.

The biblical authors share our interest in exploring various topics *as such*. For instance, what are the features of true prophecy that transcend any particular instance? Are there any ethical principles that transcend particular commands in the Torah? Less true of the Western history of philosophy, the biblical authors prescribe an examination of the nature of reality as such *through a person's groundedness in the historical and community practices of Israel.*[6]

In sum, the very first human story in the Hebrew Bible begins with an epistemological problem. The man must come to know his fit mate. Notably, coming to know does not happen through reflective exploration of the nature of the human condition, loneliness, or sexuality *as such*. Instead, he seeks to know that which YHWH already appears to know and is guided to do so through a process meant to help him discover his wife.

6. For more on this, see my essay, "Biblical Nota Bene on Philosophical Inquiry."

GENESIS 3

> Then the eyes of both were opened, and they *knew* that they were naked, and they sewed fig leaves. (Gen 3:7)

This first process of coming to know stands in stark relief to the couple's knowing of "good and evil"—an admittedly cryptic phrase in the Hebrew Bible. In order to grasp why this scene depicts egregious error, I must point out some literary features of the text along the way. These literary dimensions may seem insignificant in isolation, but taken together, they equate to a narratorial condemnation of the actions of the serpent and the couple.

In attending to the literary dimensions of the story, I also want to avoid two interpretive gaps, gaps that have had no small amount of ink spilled to fill them. The most prominent gap centers on the question: what is "knowledge of good and evil"? Is it universal knowledge? Autonomy? Moral knowledge? Or, is it merely puberty and/or sexuality, as some have suggested? I call this a gap because Scripture does not openly address this phrase. Further, I am not convinced that the story gives us enough clues to reach conclusions. In other words, the narrative presumes that knowledge of good and evil is (a) a real thing that can be had (Gen 3:7); (b) something that makes humans like YHWH (Gen 3:22); and (c) dangerous enough to require a limited lifespan with it (Gen 3:22). Outside of these, it's rarely mentioned (e.g., Deut 1:39) and never discussed. However, we can understand the impetus of the story without ever knowing exactly what the content of this knowledge is.

A lesser, though important, gap regards who added the extra-legal teaching to the command "You shall not eat of the tree." When the serpent asks, "Did God really say," the woman's response adds an extra command, "neither shall you touch it, lest you die" (Gen 3:3). From whom did she get this command?

Of course, speculation runs wild. Did the man add "neither shall you touch it" to YHWH's command as a protection? After all, if you cannot even touch the fruit, you cannot eat it. Some see this as the first *halakha*, putting a protective fence around the original command. Pragmatically speaking, it did not seem to protect her in the least. If not the man, maybe the woman inserted the addendum to the command not to eat. Or, possibly YHWH added it "off stage," as it were.

Again, I want to insist that the narrative itself is silent on both matters above. That silence can be filled with speculative stories, as some have done. Or, these two gaps might be intentional, focusing the reader on something more crucial in the story than either the nature of "knowledge of good and evil" or the blame for amending a divine instruction.

What, then, does this story focus our attention upon? Briefly, I suggest that four points help us to see why Genesis 3 is the antithesis of Genesis 2 in some crucial ways: (1) the couple's change in knowing their nakedness, (2) the woman's sight, (3) the serpent's authority, and (4) YHWH's diagnosis of the problem.

First, the story of the man's discovery (Gen 2) and the serpent's entry (Gen 3) are tied together by a rare word with two meanings. The scene of the couple's union closes with nakedness (*arum*) and a lack of shame (Gen 2:25). The very next sentence opens the scene with a serpent who was more "clever" (*arum*) than any other animal (Gen 3:1). In the same way that "blue" can describe a color, a person's mood, or something lewd, the Hebrew word *arum* can mean both naked or clever/prudent. As in all languages, the same word can take different meanings depending on the context. *Arum* shows up most frequently in the wisdom literature, meaning prudent or wise, with positive connotations. This term is rare outside of the wisdom literature. In fact, it only occurs in these two sentences in Genesis (Gen 2:25; 3:1) and then almost nowhere else from Genesis to 1 Samuel, where it is used infrequently to describe various naked people (e.g., Joseph, Gen 36:43; future exiles, Deut 28:48; Saul, 1 Sam 19:24).

Notice that at the seams of these two stories about knowing between Genesis 2 and 3, a particularly rare word that means either "naked" or "prudence" stitches the two passages together—back-to-back. *Arum* is first used as a physical descriptor—"naked"—and second, as an epistemological adjective—"crafty." This sets the reader up to understand that this story might hinge on that wordplay. Indeed, we know what changed: their knowledge of their nakedness. *What process changed the couple's knowledge of nakedness, a nakedness plainly known to the reader from Genesis 2:25?* The woman appears to see the tree differently, which affects her desire.

Second, the woman sees things differently in this short conversation with the serpent. Later, she and the man will come to a new knowledge, seeing anew their same nakedness as before. Walter Moberly offers an insightful take on this scene: "When the woman looks again at the prohibited tree, seeing it with fresh eyes in the light of the serpent's words, all she can see is that everything about it looks desirable; so why should there be a problem with it?"[7] Though not obvious, the woman's ability to see the tree under the serpent's sway is broached in Genesis 2:9, "YHWH God made to spring up *every tree that is pleasant to the sight and good for food.*" Pleasant to the sight of whom? Presumably, they are pleasant to the couple. Later, the serpent disputes

7. Moberly, *Theology of the Book of Genesis*, 80.

YHWH's threat of death by focusing her attention on her eyes being opened (Gen 3:5), knowing good and evil like YHWH himself. Notice that her seeing takes priority in leading her to act: "When the woman *saw* that the tree was good for food and that it was a delight *to the eyes* and that the tree was to be desired to make one wise," she took, she ate, and she gave some to her silent husband at hand (Gen 3:6).[8]

Her "seeing" betrays some sense of irony. In Genesis 2, *every* tree was explicitly described as both a delight to the eyes and good for food. Why does the woman now see *this one tree* as good for food and pleasing to the sight? It's difficult not to blame the serpent's interpretation for her infatuated tunnel vision of this one tree.

There are other literary indicators that she is doing something wrong, or at least, acting in extreme audacity. After all, the story does not tell you who is right or wrong in this scenario. It's only because we know the rest of YHWH's interactions that we infer his trustworthiness over the serpent's. There are, however, some linguistic clues to suspect that this story will not end well. Up to this point in Genesis, YHWH has been the only subject of the verb "to see." YHWH has repetitiously created and "saw that it was good" eight times up to this very moment. YHWH has also been the only subject—direct or implied—of the verb "take" up to now (cf. Gen 2:15, 23). When the woman *sees* the one tree differently and *takes* its fruit, the question implicit to the narrative asks: Will her seeing and taking be a good thing?

Again, the literary dimensions of the passage force us to notice the absurdity of seeing one particular tree as good and desirable. Further, the repetition of verbs—see and take—in the creation narratives heighten the tension when

8. The word "wise" here is not *arum*, rather the most common Hebrew word for "wisdom": *ḥokhmah*.

they occur in rapid succession in her actions: she saw, she took, she ate, and she gave to her husband (Gen 3:6). In the end, we are left wondering: what caused her to see that tree in that way? The most obvious candidate for that answer is: the serpent's interpretation.

Third, the text of Genesis 3 does not question the serpent's authority. Some have rightly pointed out that all three points of serpent's prediction came true precisely as he had said:

1. the couple did not die in that day (cf. Gen 2:17; 3:4);

2. they did become like God (cf. Gen 3:5, 22); and

3. their eyes were opened knowing good and evil (Gen 3:7, 22).[9]

Strangely, the narrative makes the reader more skeptical of YHWH than the serpent. What can we say about this? Not much. The serpent disappears from the biblical narrative after he receives his curses from YHWH. We do not even receive an analysis of what precisely the serpent was up to. YHWH opens his curse by alluding to the event, "Because you have *done this* . . ." (Gen 3:14). Done what? We do not know precisely. In the end, humanity sees their nakedness differently and the story indicates that their new vista is prompted by the serpent's assertions—assertions which the story in no way attempts to contradict.

This offers one significant point to consider going forward. Authoritative knowledge does not require that others should listen to the authority. The serpent clearly and accurately knew what would come of the couple's action. However, his knowledge and guidance alone are not sufficient. He must also be authenticated to them as their proper authority. The implications of this are played out later in Israel's history.

9. Moberly, "Did the Serpent Get It Right?," 1–27.

Balaam, the Moabite seer, flatly prophesies oracles that are from YHWH and against Israel's Moabite enemies (Num 22–24). However, Balaam is often depicted in the rest of Scripture as a bad character, specifically because he led Israel to intermarry and worship foreign gods. Deuteronomy supposes that prophets will be able to give authoritative knowledge about future events. However, Deuteronomy also warns Israel that not every word out of a prophet's mouth can be considered truly from YHWH (cf. Deut 13:1–3; 18:15–22). In short, authoritative knowledge—even foreseeing—does not necessitate that the authority ought to be trusted.

Fourth, and most remarkably, YHWH's questioning and diagnosis reveals a problem that cannot reduce "knowledge of good and evil" to moral knowledge or a liberating pursuit of autonomy. YHWH's only diagnosis of wrong consists of listening to the wrong voice. When YHWH enters the garden, he searches for the man (in the masculine singular). Upon finding him, YHWH asks a strange question. He does not ask the man: How did you deduce your nakedness? Or, how did you figure it out? Instead, YHWH presumes that this "knowledge," this new view of the same old data, must have involved another voice to whom they listened and obeyed. Hence, YHWH asks: "Who told you that you were naked?" (Gen 3:11).

YHWH then sets out the curses and consequences for each of the parties involved. For the serpent, YHWH begins in vagueness, "Because you have done this . . ." (Gen 3:14). For the woman, YHWH gives no reasons for her curses at all. But for the man, YHWH begins with an explanation as to what went wrong: "Because you have listened to the voice [obeyed the voice] of your wife and have eaten of the tree of which I commanded you, 'You shall not eat of it'" (Gen 3:17).

When I ask students to identify what went wrong in Eden—which some identify with the question, "When did they *sin*?"—I receive a plethora of diagnoses:

talking to the serpent at all,

entertaining the serpent's ideas,

adding to YHWH's commandment,

lusting after the fruit,

desiring autonomy,

touching the fruit,

taking the fruit,

eating the fruit,

the man's colluding with eating the fruit, or

the man's failure to correct her and/or the serpent.

Surprisingly, few students (or biblical scholars!) notice that YHWH himself indicts the man, evincing his own diagnosis of what went wrong. He says two things, but really one is just the consequence of the other: "Because you listened to the voice of your wife and have eaten . . ." (Gen 3:17). Eating comes because of listening, not listening because of eating.

This same storyline gets played over several times in Genesis with identical concepts and language. Most basically, a woman with a corrupt desire "takes" something and "gives" it to a man who "listens to the voice" of that woman. A barren Sarai pressures Abram to have children with her servant Hagar (Gen 16:1–4). Ironically, this occurs immediately after the scene where YHWH promised him as many children as the stars, which Abram "trusted" (Gen 15:6). Like the woman with the fruit, Sarai "takes" Hagar and "gives" her to Abram, and the text notes that Abram "listened to the voice of Sarai" (Gen 15:2). The language and construction of the story is so similar to the Eden narrative that some scholars have deemed "they are both accounts of a fall."[10]

Later, in the grand deceit of an aged Isaac, his wife Rebekah pressures her son Jacob to falsely commandeer the wealth and blessing from his older brother Esau. Though skeptical, Jacob complies when Rebekah pleads, "*listen to my voice* as I command you" (Gen 27:8), emphatically reiterating, "listening, listen to my voice and go . . ." (Gen 27:13). Rebekah then "takes" and "gives" Esau's garments and food to Jacob, the tools with which he can deceive his father.

Although not fitting the language precisely, Joseph acts in refreshing contrast to the patriarchs when Potiphar's wife tries to give herself to him sexually, pleading with him "day by day." Unlike Abram and Jacob, Joseph "would not listen to her" (Gen 39:10), specifically because Potiphar had "given everything that he has" into Joseph's charge (Gen 39:8).

Though this appears to be a pattern of women corrupted by their desires, this is not wholesale misogyny. In the cases of Sarai and Rebekah, John Calvin notices that both women are attempting to actualize a promise made directly from YHWH.[11] In Eden, however, the indictment cannot be leveled flatly against the woman either. When YHWH asserts, "Because you listened to the voice of your wife," by implication, the man is listening to the voice of the serpent. Hence, the "who told you" question when YHWH enters the garden (Gen 3:11).

What is YHWH's diagnosis? The man listens to—or, obeys—the wrong voice. If there is a *fall* in this story, it

10. Wenham, *Genesis* 1–15, 8. See also Berg, "Der Sündenfall Abrahams," 7–14.

11. Calvin, *Commentaries on the First Book of Moses*, 85.

clearly begins with a *shift* of trust. The couple cannot be accused of seeking autonomy in the plain sense, for they appear to "listen to" or "obey" the serpent instead of YHWH. Whatever they are doing, it begins with a trusting submission to another authority, which disqualifies it for a blatant attempt at autonomy. At worst, they seek autonomy from YHWH, but only by submitting to the serpent.

Without settling the question of sin's entry and proliferation into the universe, we can see the central idea behind knowing operative in the basic contours of the story. "Then the eyes of both were opened, and they *knew* that they were naked, and they sewed fig leaves" (Gen 3:7). Knowing is a process by which we trust authorities and embody their directions in order to know. The nakedness that was plainly known to the reading audience previously caused no shame. How do they come to see that same nakedness differently? They do what the serpent suggests and therefore come to know good and evil. Like a radiologist who sees something in an X-ray that I cannot, we look at the exact same object and, yet, she sees something different. For the radiologist, years of training, priming, and repetition under trusted knowers allow a new vista into images of the body.

This is precisely the content of YHWH's indictment: why did you trust the serpent over me? We will see in Exodus and beyond that discerning trusted authorities becomes a paramount task for the Israelites. Moses, of course, goes through the most extensive trust-inducing process imaginable with the Israelites (More than my X-ray interpreting doctor ever did with me!). Then, in light of Moses' coming death, Deuteronomy expressly prepares Israel to authenticate future prophets who claim to be authorities. We now move from examining a discrete pair of stories about knowing in Eden to a macroscopic view of knowing among entire nations and peoples in Exodus.

FOR DISCUSSION

1. Take an inventory of the areas you know best (e.g., parenting, job skill, reading emotions, etc.). How much did listening to an authority play into your knowing?

2. In this chapter, how many of the ideas about the serpent, man, woman, and God were new to you? What bothered and intrigued you the most and why?

3. Why do you suppose that figuring out "knowledge of good and evil" has consumed the effort of so many theologians? What do you do when there is a gap in the biblical story that seems to demand an explanation?

3

KNOWING IN THE EXODUS

Pharaonic and Israelite

But Pharaoh said, "Who is YHWH that I should listen to his voice to let Israel go? I do not know YHWH, and more, I will not let Israel go." (Exod 5:2)

THE EDEN STORY DEPICTS knowing as central to the story of humanity. Hence, *who* knows *what* and *how* takes center stage. The exodus story is also focused on *who* knows *what* and *how*. Specifically, Israel must come to know that YHWH—and not the other gods—is her God who liberates her from slavery so that she can worship him. Since we do not usually think of Exodus as a story about knowing, I need to make a provisionally convincing case. To make this case, I probe into the erroneous knowing of the pharaohs and the establishment of Moses as *the* trusted authority for Israel. Again, if the central idea of this book holds, I expect these texts to prioritize acknowledging and listening to the voice of a trusted authority in order to know.

THE PHARAOHS AS ERRONEOUS KNOWERS

First, the case begins in the opening sentences of Exodus: "A new king arose over Egypt who did not know Joseph" (Exod 1:8). The drama of the opening chapter erupts quickly as the Hebrews multiply and Pharaoh plans to kill the infant males.

The overarching storyline of Exodus addresses, well, the exodus! Less obvious is the repetitious return to that initial conflict: a pharaoh who does not know Joseph. Not only are the pharaohs admittedly ignorant, but we discover that Israel needs to know something as well. I call this the knowledge plot of Exodus. It can be posed alongside the liberation plot of the book, as long as we realize that the liberation functions to confirm trust in YHWH and Moses, and hence knowledge.

What does that even mean to "not know Joseph"? Similar to "knowledge of good and evil" or "knowing that YHWH is your God," knowing Joseph acts as a vague reference to the final chapters of Genesis. Not knowing Joseph appears to indict the first pharaoh's poor interpretation of Hebrew fruitfulness. The language of Exodus points to the fulfillment of Genesis 1:

> Be fruitful and multiply (Gen 1:28)

> But the people of Israel were fruitful . . . they multiplied and grew very strong (Exod 1:7)

What Genesis considers a creational good—fruitfulness—Pharaoh interprets as a looming insurgency. The one who reads from Genesis to Exodus encounters a king who does not know something, and Exodus portrays his *not knowing* through his misinterpretation of Hebrew fruitfulness.

The first pharaoh of Exodus dies and another king arises. Will this new king know Joseph, whatever that may mean? When Moses and Aaron confront the new pharaoh for the first time, we see that the problem persists. "Who is YHWH that I should listen to his voice to let Israel go? I do not know YHWH, and more, I will not let Israel go" (Exod 5:2). The language could not be more clear. The pharaoh does not know YHWH. Thus, the pharaoh will not listen to YHWH's voice. From here, we must scrutinize the text of Exodus for *relevance*: does the author care about the pharaoh's knowledge of YHWH?

Because most readers focus in on "Let my people go!" more than the repetition of "so that you will know" in Exodus, we often miss the repeated emphasis on knowing in the plague cycles. However, the reiteration of "that you will know" statements throughout the cycle of plagues makes the epistemological importance of the plagues unmistakable. Knowing appears to be part of the purpose of the plagues. Immediately prior to the first plague, YHWH summarizes the whole course of coming events: "The Egyptians *shall know* that I am YHWH, when I . . . bring out the people of Israel from among them" (Exod 7:5). To make this pattern clear, I list the plagues below, along with the italicized knowledge statements associated with them and the responses to the plagues:

1. Water to Blood
   - Moses: "By this you [Pharaoh] *shall know* that I am YHWH: . . . the Nile, and it shall turn into blood." (Exod 7:17)
   - No response from Pharaoh.

2. Frogs
   - Pharaoh's Response: "Plead with YHWH to take away the frogs . . ." (Exod 8:8)
   - Moses: "Moses said, '. . . so that you [Pharaoh] *may know* that there is no one like YHWH our God.'" (Exod 8:10)

3. Gnats

4. Flies

   - Moses: "That you [Pharaoh] may *know* that I am YHWH in the midst of the land. (Exod 8:22)

   - Pharaoh's Response: "Go sacrifice in the wilderness." (Exod 8:29)

5. Livestock

6. Boils

7. Hail

   - Moses: "So that you [Pharaoh] *may know* that there is none like me [YHWH] in all the land." (Exod 9:14)

   - Pharaoh's Response: "YHWH is in the right, I and my people are in the wrong . . . Plead with YHWH, for there has been enough of YHWH's thunder and hail. I will let you go." (Exod 9:27–28)

   - Moses: "There will be no more hail, so that you [Pharaoh] *may know* that the earth is YHWH's." (Exod 9:29)

8. Locusts

   - No response from Moses.

   - Pharaoh's Servants' Response to Pharaoh: "Let them go . . ." (Exod 10:7)

9. Darkness

   - No response from Moses.

   - Pharaoh's Response: "Go, but leave the livestock . . ." (Exod 10:24)

10. Death of the first born

    - Moses: "That you [Pharaoh] *may know* that YHWH makes a distinction between Egypt and Israel." (Exod 11:7)

    - Pharaoh's Response: "Go, but bless me also . . ." (Exod 12:32)

Upon releasing and then reneging on the Hebrews for the third time, the final act of YHWH against Egypt at the Red Sea is meant for similar epistemological effect. YHWH warns Moses that the Egyptians are coming and that he (YHWH) will "get glory of Pharaoh and his army," "and the Egyptians *shall know* that I am YHWH" (Exod 14:4). As the Pharaoh's army approach and the Hebrews fret, YHWH again tells them to go forward, for YHWH will fight for them. YHWH reiterates, "I will get glory over Pharaoh . . . and the Egyptians *shall know* that I am YHWH when I have gotten glory over Pharaoh" (Exod 14:18).

Confronted by this *present* and *persistent* pattern of YHWH's actions for the sake of knowing, it should now be clear that Exodus develops a view of knowing *relevant* to the story. Despite this epistemological interest, it is also clear that the pharaoh's knowing is central to that view. Oddly, the pharaoh does not appear to understand. More precisely, what the pharaoh understands is out of sorts with the grander reality painted by the narrator. YHWH only addresses the pharaoh's knowledge—and most of Egypt by extension—in terms of *knowing about*. Whereas YHWH intends for Israel to know that YHWH is her god, YHWH's intentions for Pharaoh are distinctly focused on knowing things *about* YHWH. Of all the instances cited above, Pharaoh is meant to know:

that I am YHWH (Exod 7:17);

that there is no one like YHWH (Exod 8:10);

that there is none like YHWH in all the land (Exod 9:14);

that the land is YHWH's (Exod 9:29);

that YHWH makes a distinction between Egypt and Israel (Exod 11:7).

If the plagues are meant to affect Pharaoh's knowing, then what aspect of his ability to know do these divine acts home in on? In other words, are they intended to change his ability to see, to give him new facts, or something else? If the biblical view of proper knowing begins with acknowledging authorities that should be trusted, then we should expect these plagues to give sufficient reasons to trust Moses' authority.

If trusting Moses and embodying his directions ought to lead Israel to know properly, then the opposite must hold as well. If Pharaoh does not acknowledge Moses' authority, then we should observe him knowing erroneously.[1] We can detect Pharaoh's convoluted knowing in two places, which are contrasted by Egyptians who do acknowledge Moses' authority.

Though the plagues were intended to "make you [Pharaoh] *see*" YHWH's power (Exod 9:16), the narrator directs our attention to what Pharaoh actually sees. We expect that Pharaoh, after so many plagues, would see that YHWH stands behind all these catastrophes. Though invisible to him, the message of these plagues means to make Pharaoh see something about YHWH through Moses' authoritative interpretation. What is Pharaoh *seeing* instead? During the plague of frogs, Exodus notes, "When Pharaoh *saw* that there was a respite, he hardened his heart and would not listen to them" (Exod 8:15).

The plague of hail exaggerates Pharaoh's myopia even further. As the hail fell, Pharaoh is only *seeing* when the hail will stop. Remember that Moses emphasized to Pharaoh before acting, "There will be no more hail, so that you [Pharaoh] *may know* that the land is YHWH's" (Exod 9:29). The narrator then reports to us, "But when Pharaoh *saw* that the

1. For the purposes of this book, I am setting aside the theological issue of YHWH's actions to harden Pharaoh's heart. I deal with this matter in *Biblical Knowing*, 73n7, 87–89.

rain and the hail and the thunder *had ceased*, he sinned yet again and hardened his heart . . ." (9:34).

In contrast to Pharaoh, some Egyptians do acknowledge Moses and listen to him. After the plague of gnats, Pharaoh's magicians claim, "This is the finger of God . . . but Pharaoh's heart was hardened and he would not listen to them" (Exod 8:19). Prior to the hail falling, Exodus notes that some of Pharaoh's servants—"whoever feared the word of YHWH"—listened to Moses' warnings and saved their livestock and slaves by sheltering them (Exod 9:20). After the locusts, Pharaoh's own servants plead with him, "Let the men go. . . . Do you not yet understand that Egypt is ruined?" (Exod 10:7). Basically, Exodus contrasts two reactions to Moses' authority: a recalcitrant Pharaoh over and against Pharaoh's defeated courtiers and servants, who have been plagued into submission to Moses' voice.

YHWH acts egregiously against Egypt so that Pharaoh would know the nature of Egypt's relationship to the Hebrews. However, like the first pharaoh of Exodus, the second pharaoh's knowledge seems out of sorts with the reality to be known. The primary cause of his erroneous knowledge is the refusal to listen to Moses. Indeed, four times Pharaoh's heart was hardened with the explicit consequence, "he would not listen" (Exod 7:13, 22; 8:15, 19).

MOSES AS THE TRUSTED AUTHORITY

Because seeing operates as a metaphor for knowing, we observe that the goal is for Israel to see truly. Specifically, Israel needs to see that it was YHWH who plagued Egypt and fights for her. In order to see YHWH behind all these events (and survive the death of the firstborn), the Hebrews must trust Moses and embody his instructions. First, it is worth considering the good reasons given to trust Moses.

Second, we learn that evidence is not self-evident. Authorities always guide us to see what is there.

Regarding the authentication of Moses, the sequence of signs leaves little room to discount the importance of being convinced. At the burning bush, YHWH tasks Moses with the exodus and Moses resists for reasons of social rank (Exod 3:11). With his first objection dismissed by YHWH, Moses then raises the most obvious objection concerning trust. Why would the Hebrews trust *him*? YHWH offers his own personal name as a token that Moses should be trusted (Exod 3:14). Despite this, Moses' skepticism is unswayed: "But behold, they will not trust me or listen to my voice" (Exod 4:1).

YHWH now embarks on a wholesale sign-and-wonder campaign, first convincing Moses (Exod 4:1–9), then Aaron (Exod 4:27–28), then the elders (Exod 4:29–30), and finally Israel (Exod 4:31). In convincing Moses, YHWH proffers signs-and-wonders by suggesting that they form the antidote to skepticism. He is to perform these signs "if they will not trust you . . . or listen to your voice" (cf. Exod 4:5, 8). Moses' skepticism is answered by a series of signs and wonders meant to first convince him that he is the authoritative voice of YHWH, and then Aaron, the elders, and the Hebrews more generally.

Both Moses and YHWH understand that gaining trust in this situation requires exceptional means of authentication. While a police badge or a doctor's ID might be sufficient to trust them as an authority in the structures of our society, Moses had no such luxury and the text admits it plainly.[2]

---

2. As an aside, I will maintain that Jesus had no such luxury either, which explains his focus on being established as the prophet of Israel along with his messianic office. The apostles also chide the "men of Israel" for the fact that convincing "signs and wonders" were provided (Acts 2:22).

The rest of the exodus narrative is spent on ensuring that the reader and the Israelites ought to acknowledge and trust Moses as the authority of YHWH. A failure to do so necessarily leads one down a road to erroneous knowing, where insight is convoluted, truncated, and out of perspective with an objective reality that could have otherwise been known truly.

Regarding the interpretation of evidence, it's all how we see it. A doctor sees the lack of arch in my feet as evinced by a bone spur. A cellist sees subtle slurs in a performance not notated in the sheet music. A detective sees a murder scene according to layers of time as well as space. I do not see any of these things, even if I observe the exact same events at the exact same time.

Hence, it simply cannot be the case that Israel, *on her own*, can be expected to see the divine actions in Exodus as originating exclusively from YHWH. In other words, a blood-brimming Nile, locusts, hailstorm, and death of one unique member of the household are not self-interpreting signs. There is nothing internal to those signs that points directly to YHWH. They all required an authority who can interpret them, attributing them appropriately to YHWH. This is not just a problem for Egypt's understanding, but Israel's too. Therefore, YHWH's promise before the plagues begin should be taken quite literally:

> I will take you to be my people, and I will be your God, and *you shall know* that I am YHWH your God, *who has brought you out from under the burdens of the Egyptians.* (Exod 6:7)

Is it possible for the Israelites to experience all those plagues, cross the Sea, and then misunderstand which god was responsible for all of that? *That is precisely what happens.* Later in Exodus, we find a few thousand people feasting and romping to the golden calf and YHWH, saying, "These are your gods, O Israel, who brought you up out of the land of Egypt" (Exod 32:4).

Indeed, the Passover ritual is geared toward ensuring that Israel would remember exactly who was responsible for the events in Egypt. Instructed in advance of the death of the firstborn, the Passover ritual both inaugurates the new calendar of Israel and annually imbues them with a living memory of exactly what happened in Egypt and who was responsible. Prior to that, during the invasion of locusts, YHWH reiterates the importance of memory-making:

> . . . that you may tell in the hearing of your son and of your grandson how I have dealt harshly with the Egyptians and what signs I have done among them, *that you may know* that I am YHWH. (Exod 10:2)

That Israel will fail this test over and over does not mitigate the clear-eyed intention of these instructions. Israel needed Moses to interpret the acts of YHWH. Israel also needed to practice YHWH's instructions of regular rituals to ensure proper knowing that would endure to her future generations.

The exodus story ends on a high note, demonstrating that Moses has been established as Israel's trusted authority, Israel has listened to Moses, and Israel has come to know YHWH as her God through the process. Prior to crossing the Red Sea, Moses explains to the Israelites what is going to happen in terms of their sight. In other words, they could all witness these events together and understand them incorrectly. Only after they have crossed the sea does the reader learn that Israel now knows because she listened to the voice of Moses. Merely comparing the identical language before and after the sea crossing reveals that the event was properly interpreted *under Moses' guidance beforehand* (Exodus 14:13–4):

> Fear not, stand firm, and *see* the salvation of
> YHWH,
> which he will work for you today.
> For the Egyptians whom you see today,
> you shall never see again.

After crossing, the narrator relays their *seeing* in symmetrical style to the prior explanation. The verbs are phrased in precisely the reverse order (Exod 14:30–31):

> and Israel saw the Egyptians dead on the
> seashore.
> Israel saw the great power
> that YHWH worked against the Egyptians,
> so the people feared YHWH, and they *trusted* in
> YHWH and in his servant Moses.

Israel saw correctly, trusting in YHWH and Moses because of it. How did they see the dead bodies and sea-splitting power as traceable to YHWH? They listened to the voice of Moses, embodied his instructions, and saw what YHWH was showing them. Hence, Israel knew truly where Pharaoh did not.

CONCLUSION

We tend to think of knowing and error as two distinct categories, you either know or you are wrong. However, these passages in Genesis and Exodus claim that even error is a case of knowing. No matter how one usurps or rejects the guided process, *everyone comes to know something.* The question presented by these stories is: Will they come to know truly or erroneously? But in the end, knowing wrongly is a form of knowing nonetheless, portrayed with exceptionally negative consequences suffered by exceptionally foolish characters.

FOR DISCUSSION

1. Why would the narrator of Exodus explicitly portray the Pharaoh's foolhardiness in repeated scenes of obstinacy?

2. Why would YHWH go to such lengths to convince Moses, Aaron, the elders, and Israel of Moses' special authority?

3. How does YHWH's willingness to convince shape our view of skepticism?

4. Can you think of any instances of self-evident truths, those which need no interpretation and are open and available for anyone to know?

4

KNOWING IN THE GOSPELS

Disciples as Dolts

On more than one occasion, I have seen two blind people walking arm-in-arm down a chock-full Manhattan sidewalk. One was clearly leading the other. In both cases, the leader used her guide stick while the other held onto her partner's arm. Quite literally, the blind was leading the blind. Neither of them was young, nor particularly nimble; but my only thought upon seeing this blind pair was: Catastrophe awaits these two!

However, as I watched them longer I noticed that they had some kind of system worked out. As a team, they had a practical way to navigate a big city. What appeared to me as a uniquely horrible combination, a blind person leading another blind person around New York City, was actually an eloquent arrangement. Physically, it was the blind leading the blind. But actually, they were more safe and "sighted" together than alone.

The gospel stories portray similarly odd affairs. Though Jesus damns the religious leaders for being "blind guides" (Matt 23:15–17), sightless men often see the true nature of Jesus' work, even when Jesus' own disciples are blind to it. Though sight is the strongest metaphor for knowing in Scripture, we have also seen a Pharaoh who *looked closely* at the facts and interpreted them all wrongly. That being so, mere sight cannot be enough, just as two merely blind people in Manhattan are not summarily doomed to catastrophe.

In continuing to examine knowing in the Scriptures, I maintain that whom we listen to forms our ability to see either correctly or convolutedly. The Eden story, the exodus, and the gospels make it clear that it's not a matter of whether we are listening to an authority. Rather, we have no choice. *By our very constitution and relationships, no matter what we do we will be listening, doing, and being shaped to see the world.* Scripture pointedly asked two questions: which voice *will* you listen to? And then, how will you embody that authority's instruction in order to see what she is showing you?

For the sake of brevity, we will consider this concept in the Gospel of Mark, and then look at similar ideas arising in Luke.[1]

THE DEUTERONOMY-ISAIAH CONNECTION

Mark crisply portrays Jesus' desire for his disciples to see "the secret of the kingdom of God" by listening to him. But the disciples thwart that desire to see because they do not listen to his instruction. Before we launch into Mark's gospel, two teachings from the Hebrew Bible must be considered: future prophets and YHWH's role in affecting the

1. I examine the narrators' perspectives on how gospel accounts function epistemologically in the Gospels of Luke and John in *Biblical Knowing*, 110–20.

heart, eyes, and ears of Israel. First, going all the way back to the Torah, the role of future prophets becomes a major crisis in Deuteronomy. Moses will die in the wilderness and Israel needs to discern who speaks for YHWH after Moses is dead. Hence Deuteronomy 13:1–5 and 18:15–22 instruct Israel to whom she should listen. The actual criteria for future prophets do not need to be rehearsed here. However, the clear use of signs and wonders along with orthodox teaching are genuine indicators of YHWH putting his words in the prophet's mouth (Deut 18:18). This teaching not only guides Israel to discern prophets who speak presumptuously, but also to heed those who speak for YHWH! What is clear in Deuteronomy's teaching, after being given the proper reasons to trust a prophet, "To him shall you listen [obey]" (Deut 18:15).

Second, the heart, eyes, and ears become metaphorical for knowing in Deuteronomy and then again in Isaiah. Specifically, Deuteronomy suggests a particular relationship between the knowing heart, seeing eyes, and listening ears. Consider how Moses chides Israel in the covenant renewal of Deuteronomy (29:2–4):

> You have seen all that YHWH did before your
> eyes in the land of Egypt,
> to Pharaoh and to all his servants and to all his
> land,
> the great trials that your eyes saw, the signs, and
> those great wonders.
> But to this day YHWH has not given you a
> heart to know or
> eyes to see or
> ears to listen.

In other words, Israel saw everything—signs and wonders—so why did Israel not understand? The surprising answer: YHWH did not give Israel a heart to know, eyes to see, or ears to listen. I would boldly suggest that these organs might even be in an order. Israel did not have a heart to know *because* she could not see what was being shown *because* she did not listen. Even the first step in knowing— listening to the trusted authority—might itself be a gift from YHWH.

What is Moses referring to by recalling the signs and wonders that Israel saw? Several instances in the book of Exodus and Numbers showed definitively that, although they had many reasons to trust Moses, Israel kept misunderstanding. These misunderstandings had fatal consequences because they did not listen diligently to Moses. Deuteronomy dredges up two instances: their worship of the golden calf while waiting for Moses at Sinai (cf. Exod 32; Deut 9:13–29) and Miriam's rebellion against Moses (cf. Numb 12; Deut 24:8–9). We could certainly name more, but these were obvious occasions with thunderously grand wonders meant to instill Israel's trust in Moses. Yet, seeing all those signs, they did not understand.

These three organs only show up in one other place *in the entire Hebrew Bible*: Isaiah's call to be a prophet.[2] Here, YHWH calls Isaiah to a terrifying vocation: truly proclaiming YHWH's oracles and instructions, which deafens and blinds Israel so that she cannot "turn and be healed" (Isa 6:9–10):

> Go, and say to this people:
> "Keep on hearing, but do not understand;
> keep on seeing, but do not perceive."
> Make the heart of this people dull,

2. Heart, eyes, and ears also show up together in Ezekiel 40:4, but in a different form. However, even in that context, the clear intent of looking with his eyes, listening with his ears, and setting his heart upon these things was "in order that I might show it to you." In other words, the context of these three organs is still epistemological.

> and their ears heavy,
> and blind their eyes;
> lest they see with their eyes,
> and listen with their ears,
> and know with their hearts,
> and turn and be healed. (Isaiah 6:9–10)

Isaiah's unenviable mission is to target the same organs of Israel with his prophecy so that his audience would be unknowing, and therefore, not healed.

Of course, in both Deuteronomy and Isaiah, the outlook is not completely bleak. In the very next teaching of Deuteronomy, YHWH promises that he himself will "circumcise your heart and the heart of your offspring." This circumcision appears to be shorthand for opening ears and eyes in order to create a knowing heart (Deut 30:6). In Isaiah, the long-range hopes for Israel are positive, leading other nations to true understanding and worship of YHWH. Isaiah later appeals: "Listen to me you stubborn of heart" (Isa 46:12), but also, "Listen to me, you who know righteousness, the people in whose heart is my torah" (Isa 51:7). Finally, Isaiah calls Israel to listen for the sake of the nations (Isa 51:4):

> Give attention to me, my people,
> and give ear to me, my nation;
> for torah will go out from me,
> and I will set my justice for a light to the peoples.

Thus, while Isaiah's call is bleak, the text cannot be understood to be completely devoid of hope *for* and *through* Israel.

Why am I talking about heart, eyes, and ears in Deuteronomy and Isaiah in a chapter on the gospels? First, despite it being a difficult teaching, it highlights a feature of biblical knowing that I have yet to address: YHWH appears to be directly involved, even when a trusted guide speaks truly. Second, Mark's Jesus uses both Isaiah 6 and Deuteronomy 29 to establish the epistemological goals for his disciples. In Mark's gospel, the disciples do not seem to fare much better than the non-listening Israelites in the Hebrew Bible: deaf to Jesus' commands, and therefore, blind to what he is trying to show them. However, we will see in Luke that opening of the eyes still happens, almost as a reversal of Eden's *shift* and *fall*. By listening to the resurrected Jesus and reinterpreting everything in light of what he instructs them, "their eyes were opened and they knew."

MARK 4–9

As usual, if you are not intimately familiar with Mark 4–9, then you should pause here and read it over.

Mark is the shortest gospel. Though it has been considered the oldest gospel in recent decades, possibly a source for Matthew and Luke, that debate does not determine what I will say here. Why look at Mark? It's not because Mark is shorter or older, but precisely because Mark has a focused use of the concepts we have been following from Genesis and Exodus. Using the language of Deuteronomy and Isaiah, Mark basically portrays the disciples as the point of Jesus' focus. Getting the disciples to understand that the crucifixion is part and parcel of the kingdom of God remains central to the narrative of Mark. Though all the gospels have a story to tell about knowing, Mark's story uniquely concentrates on the disciples. Below, I will focus my attention on one section of Mark where we see the disciples being singled out as special knowers and then following them through their successes and failures in knowing, which pointedly climax at the transfiguration account.

The Promised Mystery

The disciples' journey to knowing begins in full at the parable of the Sower (Mark 4). Jesus opens the parable with "Listen!" (Mark 4:3) and then describes seed that was thrown on various types of soil and how it fared, ending with, "He who has ears to listen, let him listen" (Mark 4:9). According to Jesus' explanation, the parable is solely concerned with whether people *listen*, and then whether they *do what they heard* (i.e., "accept it and bear fruit"; Mark 4:20). Clearly, from the parable and its interpretation, in order to see the mystery of the kingdom of God being shown to them, the disciples must acknowledge that Jesus is the trusted authority and then put his instruction into practice.

Mark uses language from Deuteronomy 29 (i.e., "ears to listen") and quotes Isaiah 6 directly. Nevertheless, Mark 4 repeatedly emphasizes "listening," yet says almost nothing about "seeing." This intense use of the verb "listen" signals to the reader that establishing Jesus as a trusted authority is the primary goal.

Later, the disciples admit to Jesus that they do not understand the parable (Mark 4:11), to which he replies with a cryptic promise: "To you all has been given the mystery of the kingdom of God" (Mark 4:10). Then he separates the disciples from everyone else quoting a slightly rearranged version of the Septuagint's Isaiah 6:

> but for those outside, everything is in parables
> so that
> "they may indeed see but not perceive,
> and may indeed hear but not understand,
> lest they should turn and be forgiven.
> (Mark 4:12)

Remarkably, Jesus actually frames his teaching with Isaiah's calling, which was meant to deafen and blind Israel.

But for the disciples, he will give them "the mystery of the kingdom of God" (Mark 4:11). That is the goal, which requires the disciples to listen to Jesus as the authority and do that which he instructs them. Unsurprisingly then, Mark concludes this passage on the subject of listening with this summary (Mark 4:33–34):

> With many such parables he spoke the word to them, *as they were able to listen.* He did not speak to them without a parable, but privately to his own disciples he explained everything.

Listening Is the Problem

How do the disciples fare in their quest to know the mystery of the kingdom of God? Not well. What was the problem? Listening and doing. That evening, in the story, they cross the Sea of Galilee. The storm arises and Jesus calms it (Mark 4:35–41). Notice the question the disciples rhetorically ask themselves in response to this wondrous event: "Who then is this, that even the wind and sea *listen to him*" (Mark 4:41). For the reader, we cannot help but ask the same of his disciples: If even the sea and wind listen to him, will you?

Moving about the region of Galilee, Jesus is dispossessing demons, healing menstruation issues, and raising the dead (Mark 5). But coming into his hometown of Nazareth, the crowds are divided between those who "listened to him" and were thus astonished by his prophetic teaching (cf. Mark 6:2, 4) and those who would not listen because he was only the carpenter's son (Mark 6:3).

He then gives his disciples authority and sends them out, two by two, to work his same wonders. Jesus notes specifically, "if any place . . . will not listen to you . . . shake the dust off of your feet" (Mark 6:11). At this point, we have high hopes for the disciples. Jesus means to reveal the mystery of the kingdom of God to these men. They are traveling along with him, seeing the wondrous signs, and are now embodying his instructions and are seeing the kingdom of God for themselves in new circumstances. Success!

The next turn in Mark's story brings both despair and wonderment. Upon their return to Jesus, they report their success. Jesus immediately isolates them, but crowds follow. Though his disciples want to send the hungry crowds away, Jesus instructs his disciples, "You all give them something to eat" (Mark 6:37). No way exists for us to determine what Jesus had in mind here. Whatever it is that Jesus wants them *to do*, they do not *do anything*. The disciples flounder and quibble about how much it would cost to feed the crowds. Then, Jesus takes the existing food and miraculously feeds the five thousand. Story seemingly over.

Incredibly, as the disciples depart by boat to the other side of the sea, Jesus catches up to their boat—walking on the water! Seeing this causes no small amount of duress amongst the disciples, but the source of their anxiety shocks the reader. Jesus climbs aboard and calms the disciples, who thought he was a ghost. But here is Mark's startling summary of that event: "And they were utterly astounded, for *they did not understand about the loaves*, but their hearts were hardened" (Mark 6:51–52).

After seeing a man walking on water, their minds were still thinking about the miraculous feeding—"for they did not understand about the loaves." Notice that Mark's gospel states it epistemologically. They did not understand, which presumes that the miraculous feeding was meant to fit into a larger pattern. Jesus had instructed them, "You all give them something to eat." Later they are perplexed about the feeding, and Mark sums it up as "their hearts were hardened." Our hopes for the disciples are diminished.

After more teaching and healing, Jesus and the disciples are again confronted with another hungry crowd, four thousand this time. Again, his disciples hedge and quibble about the impossibility of getting enough food for such a large crowd (Mark 8:4). And again, Jesus miraculously divides up the food to feed them all. No doubt exists in my mind that this next sequence until the end of Mark 8 is specifically written to make the disciples look comically foolish. Immediately after the miraculous feeding of thousands, the Pharisees come and ask for a "sign," without a hint of irony in their request (Mark 8:11–13).

Then, as if to personally place the last straw on the camel's back, the disciples discuss the fact that they forgot to bring bread on the boat. Jesus snaps. His tirade ought to now sound familiar to us and it's worth repeating in full (Mark 8:17–21):

> "Why are you discussing the fact that you have
> no bread?
> Do you not yet perceive or understand?
> Have you hardened hearts?
> Having eyes do you not see, and
> having ears do you not listen?
> And do you not remember?
> When I broke the five loaves for the five thousand, how many baskets full of broken pieces
> did you take up?"
> They said to him, "Twelve."
> "And the seven for the four thousand, how many
> baskets full of broken pieces did you take up?"
> And they said to him, "Seven."
> And he said to them, "*Do you not yet understand?*"

In this scene, Jesus scolds his disciples using the language of Isaiah 6 and Deuteronomy 29. Now the disciples appear to be the outsiders, the ones who do not listen or understand. Our hopes for the disciples plunge. But what is the essential problem here? We will see in the coming story of the transfiguration that God himself diagnoses the problem, which gives us shades of hope for the disciples, if any hope at all.

After this chastisement, a two-stage healing of a blind man (Mark 8:22–26) leads into the Christ-question, where we find out that the disciples are still not getting it. On the way to a northern city, Jesus questions his disciples, "Who do people say that I am?" (Mark 8:27). Elijah, John the Baptist, and "other prophets" are offered. When Jesus asks, "Who do *you all* say that I am," Peter instills the briefest moment of hope in the reader, saying, "You are the Christ" (Mark 8:29).

Despite the veneer of a profound epiphany, we quickly find out that a misinterpretation of "the Christ" pervades Peter's thinking. He simply cannot understand how the role of Christ could be reconciled with Jesus' forthcoming death and resurrection. Stated otherwise, Peter could not hang together the mystery of the kingdom of God with Jesus' confidence in his own dying and rising. To press the point into absolute clarity, Jesus goes further, "speaking plainly" (Mark 8:32). Not only will Jesus suffer such shame (and glory), but also everyone who follows Jesus will suffer the same (Mark 8:34–38). Peter is labeled "Satan" for opposing this plan (Mark 8:33).

This leads to the most radical and climactic moment in Mark's story apart from Jesus' death: the transfiguration. Werner Kelber describes the scene majestically:

> Structurally, its place is precisely at mid-point of the gospel. Topologically, its locale is the only "high mountain" in the gospel. Eschatologically, it stands at the turning of time toward the apocalyptic manifestation of the Kingdom.

Christologically, it comes at the peak of a titulary progression: Peter's false Christos is corrected by Jesus' suffering, rising Son of Man, to be capped by the Son of God in his parousia glory. Theologically, it marks God's only intervention outside of baptism. Dramatically, it stages God's attestation of his Son in opposition to Peter's vainglorious Christos.[3]

Only Peter, James, and John ascend the mountain with Jesus. There they see Moses and Elijah, *the* prophet of Israel and a renowned prophet respectively. Jesus is transfigured and God's voice descends to say only one thing. All of this action builds up to the hearing of God's voice and what does God say? He quotes the Greek of Deuteronomy 18 concerning future prophets of Israel: "This is my beloved son, *to him shall you listen*" (Mark 9:7).[4] Hence, Joel Marcus sums up this scene:

> On the one hand, this divine acclamation implies Jesus' continuity with Moses and Elijah, since "listen to him" echoes Moses' own words about the arising of a prophet like himself (Deut. 18:15, 18), an oracle that by the first century was being read eschatologically.
>
> On the other hand, however, the voice designates only one of the three personages, Jesus, as God's Son, and this is a title that hints at an identity greater than that of Moses or Elijah.[5]

3. Kelber, *Kingdom in Mark*, 85.

4. The instruction "to him you shall listen" in Mark 9:7 is regarded as a "virtual citation" from Deuteronomy 18:15 concerning the future prophets of Israel. See Marcus, *Way of the Lord*, 81; Menken and Moyise, *Deuteronomy in the New Testament*, 37–8.

5. Marcus, *Mark 8–16*, 640. John Calvin takes this view, as well: *Commentary on a Harmony of the Evangelists*, 191.

By the time we reach Mark 9, we are almost to the final week of Jesus' life. The disciples have repeatedly witnessed and personally participated in the miraculous work of Jesus. *Why does God, who chooses to say just one thing, need to remind them to listen to Jesus?* The presumption appears to be that the disciples do not actually esteem Jesus as *the* prophet of Israel.

Most basically, Jesus' transfiguration and God's command to listen only make sense if the disciples are floundering on this point. Even if they sometimes heed his words and put them into practice, his prior chastisement—Have your hearts hardened?—indicates that the matter is by no means settled. After the transfiguration, Mark continues to portray the disciples as dolts. In the coming chapters, the disciples argued about who is the greatest disciple among them (Mark 9:33–37), they wrongfully rebuke children approaching Jesus (Mark 10:13–16), some blindly make power grabs in the future kingdom (Mark 11:35–45), and some betray or deny Jesus during the Passion Week (Mark 14:43–72). If we allow only the short ending of Mark,[6] one centurion (Mark 15:39) and a handful of women (Mark 16:1–8) are the only persons who actually know about Jesus' resurrection.

In the end, Mark's gospel leaves the reader holding onto thin shreds of hope that the disciples will ever grasp what Jesus was trying to show them. Even that shred is premised upon the conviction that because Jesus tried, the apostles should somehow come to know what he was showing them. But in itself, Mark offers little insight into whether the disciples understood the mystery of the kingdom of God, a topic later clarified in the book of Acts. Conversely, Mark

6. The "short ending" of Mark presumes that the shortest manuscripts are the oldest, which puts the ending of Mark's gospel at Mark 16:8.

unabashedly offers a stark picture of persons who were meant to know this mystery, yet were blind to it because they did not acknowledge and heed the instruction of Jesus.

Irony & Foreshadowing: The Blind Will See

While the disciples are specifically meant to understand this mystery of the kingdom of God, they do not appear to understand. Yet, two blind persons in Mark's gospel actually seem to grasp that Jesus is the authority to be trusted. Mark contains only two blind healings and both of them appear to represent some aspect of the disciples' knowledge.

First, immediately after Jesus' chastisement of the disciples and prior to Peter's assertion that Jesus is the Christ, an odd healing juts out of the story (Mark 8:22–26). Indeed, the healing of the blind man at Bethsaida is the only one of its kind in all the gospels. Jesus heals the man in two stages. The first attempt to heal moves him from blind to blurry vision—"I see men, but they look like trees walking" (Mark 8:24). The second attempt moves him from blurry to seeing everything "clearly" (Mark 8:25).

Why does Jesus heal the man in stages? One answer asserts that the man's vision represents the disciples: currently blind. As they follow Jesus and do what he says, the mystery of the kingdom of God comes into view blurrily, only revealing its contours. At some point, something must happen to clarify their vision. There is debate about whether or not the disciples ever get clear vision within Mark's gospel itself. It might be the case that clarity does not come until Pentecost, the first time in the New Testament where we can confidently assert, "Peter understands."

Literarily, this healing episode occurs right before Peter's empty confession that Jesus is the Christ. This might be the moment when Peter moves from blind to blurried vision of the kingdom mystery. That would be an uncontroversial reading. However, less obvious is the point when Peter moves from blurry to clear vision in Mark.

Second, after the transfiguration, the Sons of Zebedee make a bold request. "Teacher, we want you to do for us whatever we ask of you" (Mark 10:35). Jesus questions them, "What do you want me to do for you" (Mark 10:36). They ask for eminent positions in this new kingdom, sitting at Jesus' right and left sides. Jesus then lectures the two brothers on their inability to undergo what he must in order to be "in glory." Above all else, the whole episode serves to underline how much they do not understand about the mystery of the kingdom of God.

Conversely, the very next sentence opens the scene at Jericho where we find blind Bartimaeus begging. Notice that Jesus asks Bartimaeus the identical question that he posed to the Sons of Zebedee: "What do you want me to do for you" (cf. Mark 10:36, 51). Bartimaeus answers, "My master, let me recover my sight" (Mark 10:51). Jesus commends him, "Go your way, your trust (*pistis*) has made you well" (Mark 10:52).

The stark contrast could not be plainer to the reader. The brothers want positional authority while naively thinking they can earn it. Even more, they open with a foolish request "to do for us whatever we want." Their ambition seeks to domesticate Jesus' plans for the kingdom. Yet, Bartimaeus addresses Jesus as "*my* master (*rabbouni*)" and only seeks to regain what was lost: his natural sight.

It's genuinely difficult to understand this second healing as anything but a critique of the sons of Zebedee. The ones who saw the transfiguration with their own eyes now naively seek to have an eminent share of the future kingdom. While the one who cannot see at all, hopes to regain his natural ability now lost. Jesus rebukes the former for their desires and commends the latter for his trust. Ironically, the blind man sees what is opaque to at least some of the disciples.

Hope for the Hapless?

Mark's gospel demonstrates the central idea we have been following thus far. In order to know, even to make sense of a pattern called the kingdom of God, the disciples must listen to Jesus' voice, embody his instruction, and focus on what he is showing them. To the extent that they listen and do, the gospel paints them favorably. To the extent they do not trust Jesus' authority or do not do what he says, which is the majority of the time, Mark depicts them as blind and hard-hearted.

What are we to make of the disciples' journey to knowing in Mark's gospel? Debate about whether Mark is a negative gospel or not—fundamentally pessimistic about the efficacy of Jesus' work and the disciples' understand-ing—will persist. Mark uses Isaiah and Deuteronomy as a template for the disciples' responses, and so the author must have some hope for people to be given a heart to know, eyes to see, and ears to hear. The disciples do make progress, no matter how minimal or slow. Unless the whole gospel is essentially defeatist, then we must presume that, like Deuteronomy and Isaiah, those who are currently deaf and blind to God's plans are not necessarily precluded from ever coming to know.

LUKE 24

> She *took* of its fruit and ate, and she also *gave* some to her husband who was with her, and he ate. Then *the eyes of both were opened, and they knew* that they were naked. (Genesis 3:6–7)

With all the doom and gloom of Mark behind us, I want to close this discussion with the prospects offered to us by Luke. Luke's gospel gives us direct hope, even while drawing an equally hapless portrait of the disciples.

Peculiar to Luke, his opening words begin with an epistemological premise. He wants his reading audience to confidently know the things they have heard (Luke 1:4). He acknowledges that other gospel accounts exist, but that he has compiled an orderly account from the witnesses of the events (Luke 1:2).

At the end of Luke, after the resurrection, we find another peculiar feature of his gospel. Luke alone tells of two disciples on their way to Emmaus (Luke 24:13–35). In this story, the two disciples attempt to hang all the pieces of recent events together (Luke 24:14). Discussing "all these things that had happened," they try to understand the mysterious kingdom of God. As they went, the resurrected Jesus comes along with them. As with most resurrection narratives in the gospels, these two do not recognize Jesus. Unlike the other gospels, though, Luke tells us *why* they could not identify the man as Jesus: "their eyes were kept from recognizing him" (Luke 24:17).

According to Luke, these two revered Jesus as a mighty prophet (Luke 24:19). Further, they seem to have integrated Jesus' teaching into the events at hand. However, they cannot reconcile his death with their hopes for the one meant to "redeem Israel" (Luke 24:21). We have ideal knowers in this situation, men who listened closely to Jesus and presumably acted upon some of his instruction. Now, they still cannot see how it all fits together.

Jesus, as he is wont to do, takes these two to task, identifying their hearts as the problem (Luke 24:25–26):

> "O foolish ones, and *slow of heart* to trust all that
> the prophets have spoken! Was it not necessary

that the Christ should suffer these things and
enter into his glory?" And beginning with Moses
and all the Prophets, he interpreted to them in all
the Scriptures the things concerning himself.

Again, even though Jesus is the trusted authority who
is over their shoulders, as it were, explaining the messiah
through the Torah and Prophets, they still do not see how
Jesus' death fits with their messianic hopes.

What bridges the gap between the disciples seeing
or not that Jesus' death and resurrection are part of the
kingdom of God? A ritual. Luke stays our hopes that the
disciples will *get it* until they have arrived and are seated
for a meal. Only when Jesus ritually takes the bread, blesses
it, and gives it to them does the narrator relieve the tension: "And their eyes were opened and they knew him"
(Luke 24:31). In Polanyi's words, they gained "a foothold at
another shore of reality."[7] Though something kept their eyes
from knowing Jesus at the beginning of the story, something or someone also opened their eyes at the end.

Moreover, they both acknowledge their internal sense
that a process of coming to know was happening: "Did not
our hearts burn within us while he talked to us on the road,
while he opened to us the Scriptures?" (Luke 24:32). They
both also acknowledge that Jesus was the authority who
coached them to see. However—the narrator is clear on
this point—the disciples were passive both when they were
kept from knowing Jesus and when their eyes were finally
opened.

The similarities to the eating of fruit in Eden are
unmistakable. In both cases, food is the object that somehow enables changed vision. In both cases, food is specifically *taken* and *given*. In both cases the action subsequently
causes the eyes to be opened with the result, "they knew."

7. Polanyi, *Personal Knowledge*, 123.

In fact, Luke is directly quoting the Greek translation of Genesis 3:7 here.

Expected by no one, Luke closes his gospel with a reversal of Eden. Using the seeing eyes as a metaphor for understanding, Luke calls our attention back to the very first problem in knowing (Gen 3:6), and then flips it. Instead of listening to the wrong voice, they listen to the voice whom they should trust. Instead of knowing their nakedness, they now know the plan of God from Moses to Jesus and beyond. Instead of knowledge causing them to squirrel away in shame, they exuberantly go out to the others and make it known: "The Lord has risen indeed" (Luke 24:34). This kind of knowing is something worth spreading, not hoarding and hiding.

FOR DISCUSSION

1. What do you make of the disciples' collective witlessness throughout most of the gospels? What does this say about the teaching ability of Jesus?

2. Why would Jesus cite Isaiah 6 in reference to his plans for the disciples? Is it not unfair that Jesus would purposely blind people from the truth? How does this contradict some popular notions about Jesus' message and work?

3. If the disciples on the road to Emmaus are a type of reversal of the Fall, do we share any hope in that event at Emmaus?

5

KNOWING THROUGH RITUAL

Rite to Know

To KNOW, I MUST do. Unlike Scout Finch, I remember well the summer that I learned to read biblical Hebrew. In order to know the language of Hebrew, I attended a ritually structured class, where we recited verb paradigms by rote over and over. Eventually, by participating in a strange collection of embodied rituals (e.g., writing exercises, oral practice, explanation, community reflection on English grammar, etc.) under the expert guidance of a professor, those strange marks seemed to be changing. They were no longer a series of cryptic symbols. The diagram below attempts to represent what Hebrew looked like to me before learning it (on the left): an enigmatic wall of symbols. But through the rituals of language learning, those symbols became words, and later, comprehensible sentences (on the right).

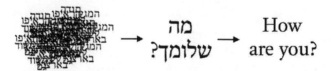

In reality, the Hebrew words never changed. I was the one who changed. I became someone who knew Hebrew. The words remained the same, but my ability to see them as words with meaning was transformed. *So, what changed*

me? It was not information. No amount of information would have bridged the gap between me *not* knowing Hebrew and knowing Hebrew. Like Scout Finch's learning to read, there *was* a magical time where the words came alive to me, though I clearly remembered when it began to happen. The transformation that enabled me to know Hebrew was a series of practices that I had to embody under the guidance of an authority. At some point, I crossed over to that other shore of reality. I had a series of epiphanies, which led to a knack for reading Hebrew. At some point, when the knack or skill is acquired, the training wheels came off and I "just knew."

In this chapter, I want to examine the reasons why ritual practices lead us to know, rather than transfer information to us.[1] The Hebrew Bible and Christian Scriptures presume a thoroughly *ritualed* life for the sake of knowing correctly. First, the rituals of Scripture are mostly normal human practices. Hence, we ought to consider why normal activities are sometimes considered special. Second, rituals are often assumed to symbolically represent what people are thinking, or what they should be thinking. However, what if rituals are not primarily about the symbols or signs? Third, I want to show that the Hebrew Bible and New Testament both develop an idea that rituals are for the sake of knowing—seeing the same data differently, as it were.

What is the relationship between rituals and knowing in Scripture? Among other goals, Israel's rituals were intended to bring Israelites to know *something*. The Hebrew Bible portrays Israelites as logically separated from knowing that which they need to know apart from their participation in its specified rituals. For their part, the Christian Scriptures presume that ritual knowing remains the norm.

1. This chapter represents an extraordinarily brief summary of Dru Johnson, *Knowledge by Ritual*.

In short, if Israel listens to the prophets, then rituals are part of what they prescribe for Israel *to do* in order to see what they are showing her.

RITUAL THEORY, RITUAL KNOWING

Consider the ritual of giving diplomas for college graduations. How does a fancy piece of paper (i.e., a diploma) confer years of work and a title onto a person? Generally, we think that the paper represents the whole course of work that leads to the title (e.g., PhD). But even then, the paper has been ritualistically engraved (e.g., a signature), ritual participants dress in gaudy costume, flourished speeches are made, and sometimes prayers to the deity are offered. Families usually attend the rite and offer up a ritual feast afterward. In analyzing what humans think they are doing in a graduation ceremony, we can get stuck on certain behaviors and practices. Of course, the ceremony tends to climax at the giving of the diploma, the sign that fully represents the work, its evaluation, and the "rights and responsibilities" that come with a diploma.

Ironically, in very large university graduations, even the symbol of graduation is replaced with a form letter stating that the diploma itself will arrive later in the mail once all academic work has been assessed, confirmed, and most importantly, *all fees have been paid*. Hence, the very symbol of graduation—the diploma—is replaced with another symbolic placeholder—the letter of promise.

If we believe that rituals are symbolic of internal thoughts, then the diploma's role in the ritual of graduation primarily acts as a signal, pointing to the successful completion of required education. We often interpret the events at a graduation by understanding the symbolic meaning of the diploma, the robes, the procession, the music, etc. These symbols supposedly point us back to the thinking behind the symbols—the things they intend to represent and the relationship of those symbols in the ceremony.

Ritual of the Graduation	:: Meaning behind the ritual?
Robes	:: Identifying and elevating the degree grantee?
Processional marching	:: Orderliness?
Colored tassels	:: Represents college or degree program?
Family presence	:: Important rite of passage?
Words of conferral	:: Represents official transcripts?

But, this obviously does not work with the graduation ceremony. No amount of symbolism and practice of this ritual will help one to understand precisely what is going on in that ritual. What do graduation robes, hats, maces, and ropes symbolize? In other words, how do the practices in the left column above act as one coherent ritual that can be translated into meaning in the right column? For instance, in what way is a graduate's gown and mortar-boarded cap related to the college experience, diploma, conferral, etc.? How does that garb fit into or explain the reasoning behind the ceremony? If it's a symbol, then it represents something and what it represents is related to other representative symbols present in the graduation. What we find when analyzing the logic of graduation rites is that they are funded mainly from tradition more than convey a symbolic logic of graduation. The lack of logic between the elements in a graduation creates difficulties for us. Perhaps, I could clarify this point by comparing the interpretation of graduation rituals to the interpretation of parables.

Parables are meant to have symbolic meaning too. And, the symbols are directly and logically related to each other, representing the reality to which the parable points. So when Jesus teaches about a man who did not count the cost of building the tower ahead of time (Luke 14:28–33), we realize that the man, the tower, and the failure to anticipate costs are all directly symbolic of another reality where those elements are logically related to each other. The logic of that parable could be shown this way:

World of the Parable	:: *Actual World*
Man	:: Disciple
Building costs	:: Costs of discipleship (financial and other)
Tower (carrying plan to completion)	:: Following Jesus (all the way to the end)

In parables, part of the strategy of symbolism is to show the relationship in the fictional world of the parable to identical relationships in the actual world. So the primary goal is to decode the symbols—figuring out who is the prodigal son, the unworthy servant, or the naïve tower-builder—in order to understand the real world being described. In other words, the parable's encoded symbolism directly represents something else.

Many interpret biblical rituals this way too, supposing that rituals are just living parables. They have symbols in relationships. The primary goal in understanding the ritual is to decode the symbols and then the hidden world of ancient Israelite theology will be revealed to us. However, this all presumes that the ritual is the outward expression of the inner thought life of Israel's prophets, or even YHWH himself.

I want to suggest that this approach mishandles the biblical teaching on rituals. Rituals are not the outward expression of inner thought; at least they are not merely that. Neither are rituals created merely to solve a problem (e.g., sin offering solves the problem of immoral behavior), as many ritual theorists suppose. *Rather, rituals are the authoritative instructions of the prophets meant to be listened to and practiced so that Israel might know what YHWH is trying to show her.*

Anthropologist Catherine Bell argues that a fundamental misunderstanding of ritual has dominated our thinking in the West.[2] She claims that we see rituals as primarily symbolic expressions of beliefs in the minds of the participants—like parables. Hence, ritual is fundamentally about what we think because our rituals are symbolically expressing our thoughts. Under this misunderstanding, ritual is a thinking man's game. Actions represent thoughts directly through signs and symbols. Yet, presuming that rituals are only actions-expressing-thought might distort what happens by participating in ritual. For Christians, the view that ritual actions merely express inward thoughts excludes what the Scriptures plainly report, that at least some of Israel's rituals—if not all of them—are meant to shape knowers and not merely express what is already believed or known.

Bell identifies the problem in our understanding as the "thinking-acting dichotomy." That is, because we think, we therefore act. Although this idea seems so basic as to be common sense, it hides several pitfalls (see below). Various developments in twentieth-century scholarship have also

2. Bell, *Ritual Theory, Ritual Practice.*

attacked this thinking-acting dichotomy. Philosophers—
mostly phenomenologists—argued for the value of human
experience as philosophically important. Because one
experiences the world differently as a blind man, a dou-
ble-amputee, or a woman, her first-person experience actually does matter to any philosophical explanation of reality.
Once presumed to be secondary or accidental to human
rationality, the body has also been reevaluated as pivotal for
human reason itself.[3] The feminist critique caused a broad
reappraisal of the body as integral to thought—not merely
expressing it.[4] Basically, the body's fundamental importance in knowing has had a rigorous and growing defense
from the mid-twentieth century to the present.

If ritual participants are not just thinkers who act—
where thoughts and actions can be easily separated from
each other—how are rituals a kind of thinking, rather than
mere expressions of thought? Two problems immediately
confront us: normal human acts can become rituals and
ritual is aimed at knowing.

First, we must describe rituals so that we can tell the
difference between normal non-ritual activity and special
ritual behavior. For instance, when does bathing become
baptism? When does butchering an animal for meat become sacrifice? When does a meal become Communion? It
is not always obvious what rituals are, as opposed to ordinary human practices.

The problem of differentiating rituals from normal
practices does not evaporate by observing current rather
than ancient rituals. Today, Western omnivores like me

3. Lakoff and Johnson, *Metaphors We Live By*. For precise examples from mathematics, *see*: Lakoff, *Women, Fire, and Dangerous
Things*, 353–69.

4. The insights of Phyllis Trible, among many others, have been
particularly helpful here. *God and the Rhetoric of Sexuality*.

participate—either directly or through my butcher—in slaughtering animals more than the ancients could have ever imagined. What makes a modern slaughterhouse different than the slaughter activities at the Herodian Temple in Jerusalem, for instance?

Bell answers this problem by developing the view she calls "ritualized practice." By "ritualized," she means to overcome the thinking-acting dichotomy. Seen as *ritualized practice*, the question of rituals is not "What belief does this ritual express?" Rather, we ask, "Why was this common practice of animal slaughter, eating a meal, or bathing appropriated to serve as a ritual?" Further, "How does this *ritualized practice* shape the participant to understand her reality differently?" Or, how does it change her view of the same old data?

Second, although ritual theory has helpfully adjusted away from the "thinking-acting dichotomy," less attention has been paid to how ritual might form our knowledge by means of participation. While ritual is not always aimed at one goal, a ritual can have complex outcomes, one of which is knowing. Bell demonstrates how ritual produces conceptual knowledge through the act of required kneeling during prayer:

> Required kneeling does not merely *communicate* subordination to the kneeler. For all intents and purposes, kneeling produces a subordinated kneeler in and through the act itself . . . we see an act of production—the production of a ritualized agent able to wield physically a scheme of subordination or insubordination.[5]

The ritual provides the concept through its embodiment. In other words, if one does not kneel, they will not

---

5. Bell, *Ritual Theory, Ritual Practice*, 100, italics original.

be able to conceptualize *subordination* in the particular way being prescribed.

In order to examine the biblical rituals, as they are presented to us in the Hebrew Bible and New Testament, we need a rich account of knowing. The robust view of human knowing found in Genesis, Exodus, and the Gospels aptly critiques the idea that "rituals merely express beliefs." With Catherine Bell, I am skeptical that the thinking-acting dichotomy best captures the meaning of rituals. However, I will need to show why my view that "rituals make knowers" fits the biblical texts best. Let us now consider a few lively examples of ritually induced knowing from Scripture.

RITUAL AND KNOWING IN THE HEBREW BIBLE

The Hebrew Bible repeatedly depicts rituals as epistemological. For instance, the express goal of tent-living seven days during Sukkot (Feast of Booths) is so that Israel's generations would know that YHWH made Israel to live in booths during their flight from Egypt (Lev 23:41). By recounting the story to the children, Israelites can make known the bare fact of tent-living to their children. However, a different goal emerges in the biblical text: knowing something *about* tent-living during the exodus. That something-to-be-known can only be known *through* tent-living. Because Scripture does not focus on a product called knowledge, I will follow its lead—focusing instead on its curious insistence that a logical gap exists between knowing and not knowing. That gap can only be bridged by participation in a ritual prescribed by YHWH or his prophet.

Genesis 15: Doubt Answered by Ritual

In Genesis 15, YHWH restates his covenant to Abram. First, YHWH promises children, as numerous as the stars. Abram trusts God for this incredible feat and his trust is counted to him as righteousness—whatever this may mean (Gen 15:6). To put it simply, an implausible promise is offered, Abram responds in trust, and God reciprocates with recognition of Abram's trust. Second, YHWH promises land, what turns out to be the entire Fertile Crescent, as Abram's inheritance. Abram questions YHWH in vocal disbelief: "How *shall I know* that I shall possess it" (Gen 15:8). YHWH's answer to the question challenges many modern assumptions about knowledge. His answer presupposes a known animal sacrifice (Gen 15:9–10). Abram appears to understand that he is participating in a covenant-making ritual.[6] The exact nature of this ritual, bizarre as it might seem to us, is not important for the current task. I have argued above that this ritual does not merely present symbols in a coded relationship. Therefore, decoding the meaning of each animal will not help us to understand the meaning of the rite.

We must notice, however, that YHWH answers Abram's incredulity ("How shall I know?") with a ritual. In case we were in doubt that the ritual is explicitly for the sake of Abram's knowing, YHWH repeats Abram's words of doubt in his pronouncement during the rite: "Knowing, you shall know . . ." (Gen 15:13). We need not investigate how cutting animals in half and arranging them produces knowledge in Abram in order to see that the ritual is meant for Abram to know something, even through limited participation.

---

6. If Kline is correct, Abram's nonparticipation in passing through the pieces of animal appears to be a modification of a treaty where normally, both parties would pass through. Kline, *By Oath Consigned*, 17–21.

Ceremonial Knowledge: Sabbath and Sukkot

While much of the current scholarship on knowledge still centers on knowing facts (e.g., knowing that "H_2O is the chemical depiction of the molecule 'water'"), the Hebrew Bible commands that *festivals* be celebrated for epistemological reasons. Notably, this knowledge cannot be stated as a fact about the world. For instance, the day of Sabbath is ritualized, set apart, and strategically practiced to be unlike all the other days of the week. Moses instructs Israel concerning Sabbath: "Nevertheless, you must keep my Sabbaths, for this is a sign between me and you throughout the ages, *that you may know* that I YHWH have sanctified you" (Exod 31:13). Again, we do not need a detailed account of either Sabbath or sanctification in order to see that the phrase "that you may know" depends upon Israel's Sabbath-keeping.

As was mentioned above, Leviticus indicates that Israel should keep the practice of sleeping in booths during Sukkot "*in order that the generations may know* that I made the sons of Israel live in booths when I brought them out of the land of Egypt" (Lev 23:43). Deuteronomy reinforces the thrust of the festival to enable knowing, emphasizing that Sukkot is for Israel's children "who *have not known . . .*" (Deut 31:13).

These examples broach a fundamental question: If Israel were meant to know facts—"consecration by God means X," "sanctification means X," or "that Israel once lived in booths"—then why perform the prescribed actions of Sabbath rest or booth-living? Stated otherwise, if these are mere facts to be known, *why cannot Israelites verbally pass along the facts to each other and their children?*

One plausible suggestion is that Israel is meant to know something *about* the fact that YHWH has consecrated her. There is some way in which Israel needs to discern *that* information beyond mere recognition. Some insights can only be gained by performing the festivals and Sabbaths. By doing these things, they will see Israel's history differently, just as I see the night sky differently than the skilled sight of the astronomer. In brief, the festival rites presume that mere knowledge of the fact is insufficient. The knowledge desired by YHWH requires embodied participation in order to see the history of Israel truly. Merely *knowing that* Israel was made to live in booths does not bridge the gap between what Israel now knows and what her generations need to know—the special significance of this history. We can now see that at least some rituals of Israel have a clear epistemological impetus (e.g., "knowing you will know"; Gen 15:13) and goal (e.g., "so that you will know"; Lev 23:43).

Testing to See

One final episode from the Hebrew Bible will be instructive for developing the view that not all acts of knowing are of the same quality. God tests Israel and Israelites test God in order to know something about each other. The narrator of Judges claims that God "might test" Israel because they did not know the wars of prior generations (Judg 3:1–2). The purpose of the test is stated unambiguously, "to know whether they would listen to the commandments . . ." (Judg 3:4). The text portrays God as needing to *recognize* something about Israel, something foundational for discerning what kind of people they were. God is in the position of the teacher who subjects his students to examination in order to recognize patterns in their behavior (e.g., Are they the kind of people who will generally trust Moses' teaching because of their parents' instruction?).

The narrator presumes that the presence of the Philistines and Canaanites in the land tests Israel about her *ritualized practices*. Performing rituals not instructed in the

Torah results in Israel's ability to recognize or not. In other words, whose rituals this new generation practiced reveals their location on the spectrum of knowing: blind to reality, basically able to recognize, or having wise discernment.

These divine tests are not unique to Judges. We see the same goal stated in the binding of Isaac. Genesis 22 tells us, "After these things it happened that God put Abraham to the test" (Gen 22:1). When Abraham prepared to kill Isaac, the angel of YHWH announced that recognition was achieved: "for now I know that you fear God" (Gen 22:12). The implications are patent: God needed to recognize something about Abraham and it required a ritual *in order for God to know*. Without getting into matters of God's actual knowledge, this is how the text reports YHWH's process of knowing to us.

The above passages were meant to demonstrate the varied use of ritual for the sake of knowing in the Hebrew Bible. We could also mention other ritualized encounters for the sake of knowledge, such as Passover (Exod 12) and stone memorials (Josh 4). However, these will have to suffice as examples, meant to be just that—examples that demand further investigation.

RITUAL KNOWING IN THE EARLY CHRISTIAN COMMUNITY

Unless we have reasons to suspect otherwise, silence concerning rituals will be considered as an indication that they continued. Stated otherwise, because the New Testament authors and much of their audiences were Jews, unless I have good reasons to suspect that they were overthrowing the Torah's rituals, I presume they continued in some way. I also presume that some biblical authors, being first-century Jews, (e.g., James, John, Peter, Paul, Matthew) would have participated in temple-centered worship and reading of the Torah as did their peers. Indeed, Paul directly participates in temple animal sacrifice rituals during his very last days in Jerusalem for the sake of proving his Torah-centered approach to the gospel (Acts 21:17–26).

That being said, does the New Testament as a whole have a negative view of ritual? Recently, several scholars have demonstrated the anti-ritual tendency that affects large swaths of biblical scholarship.[7] Basically, readers presume that ritual is rote, not related to reason, and therefore, not helpful in knowing. Or, rituals are premised upon magic, a transaction of *doing* something in order to *get* something in return. These kinds of biases overlook the way in which rites produce a certain kind of knower. A palpable distaste for the killing of animals as a type of YHWH worship might have also skewed decades of scholarship. Because we moderns are often averse to the idea of animal sacrifice, seeing it as unnecessary violence, it hinders us from thinking clearly about what these texts are describing and what they could have meant to the ancient practitioners. Ironically, we treat the modern and copious sacrifice of animals for general consumption with ambivalence. As Wesley Bergen notes, "In our society, the problem is compounded because we react in horror to the killing of animals [in the Biblical texts], yet happily consume meat in quantities unheard of in the ancient world."[8]

We need to approach the biblical texts with the presumption that rituals shape knowing, as much as or more than verbal debates in the early Jewish-Christian community. If the New Testament has a positive view of ritual— that rites have an active function in the early Jewish Jesus

7. Klawans, *Purity, Sacrifice, and the Temple*, 32, 114. Douglas, *Purity and Danger*, 18–19, 62–63.

8. Bergen, "Studying Ancient Israelite Ritual," 579–86.

movement—can we still see the vestiges of Torah rites linked to knowing in Christian Scripture? Though we cannot pursue that question in full, a few examples will help to make a basic case.

Ritual participation appears presumed rather than discussed in the New Testament. For instance, the Jewish practice of baptism appears without comment in the Gospels as a normal ritual act. The festivals and Sabbath appear only in the background of the central stories of the Gospels, coming to the foreground in points of conflict.[9] I believe Jonathan Klawans is correct when he summarizes the data from the New Testament: "Jesus' followers did not separate themselves from the temple and its sacrificial worship."[10] With this in mind, I will make a brief case that the scripted rituals in the New Testament are new Jewish rituals that retain the goal of knowing.

Luke and Rituals

The New Testament texts maintain a generally positive description of ritual. I can only point to a few highlights here. First, in Luke, the temple is the place of divine communication. John the Baptist's father is a Levite serving on rotation in the temple when he has a vision in the Holy Place (Luke 1:5–25). John the Baptist is later circumcised and Jesus presented at the temple for Mary's post-birth purification "according to the law of Moses" (Luke 2:22–24). Luke even quotes the passage from Exodus (Exod 13:2, 12) and Leviticus (Lev 12:8) concerning the precise animal sacrifice brought on behalf of her purification: two birds. Anna, the prophetess, is described as a woman of the

9. E.g., Jesus' disciples processing grain on the Sabbath (Luke 6:1–5), delay in visiting the tomb of Jesus due to keeping Sabbath (Matt 28:1).

10. Klawans, *Purity, Sacrifice, and the Temple*, 217.

temple, fasting and praying there night and day (Luke 2:36–38). The summary of the birth narrative in Luke ends with a full affirmation of their ritual life: "And when they had performed everything according to the Torah of the Lord, they returned to Galilee" (Luke 2:39). The one slice of Jesus' life completely obscured in the other gospels—Jesus' childhood—is fleetingly depicted in reference to the pilgrimage and animal sacrifice of Passover (Luke 2:41–51).

Second, Luke recounts John's baptism in terms of knowing. In recalling John's prophetic authority, Luke notes that those who understood John were the ones whom John had previously baptized. However, those who were undiscerning (i.e., the Pharisees and the lawyers), "rejected the purpose of God not having been baptized by him" (Luke 7:29–30). At the very least, some connection between discernment and baptism exists in Luke, even if only to denote the ones who understand apart from those who do not.

As for rituals themselves, Luke does nothing to discourage the reader from thinking about this new Jewish sect, later called Christianity, in terms of Israelite ritual practices. At the inauguration of Jesus' public ministry with John the Baptist, Levitical water rituals have been moved to the Jordan River as preparation for the messiah (Luke 3:1–21). Upon healing the ten lepers, Jesus sends them to the priests to perform their sacrifices and rites of purification, which would include Levitical baptism (Luke 17:11–19). Upon "cleansing" the temple courts of commerce, Jesus then begins to teach in the temple, which is where he was instructed as a child (cf. Luke 2:41–52; 19:45–48). Although Jesus prophesies the destruction of the temple, he appears to consider that a sad but necessary event (cf. 21:5–9; 19:41–44). Finally, in Luke, Jesus participates in animal sacrifice during Passover (Luke 22:7).[11]

11. To what extent he directly participates is unknown, but

Luke makes no effort to hide the fact that Jesus and his family are full participants in the rituals of Israel with positive descriptions of the rites and the Torah throughout. Like the prophets, Jesus singles out the abuse of rituals for critique, but continues to pursue their proper use.

Acts and Rituals

The narrative of Acts continues the trend of Luke's positive treatment of Torah ritual. While it certainly creates a perplexing relationship between Israelite rituals and the Gentiles (e.g., circumcision), Luke does not downplay the centrality of the temple rites for the early church as long as the temple is still standing. The seminal event of Acts—the Holy Spirit at Pentecost—is predicated by the *Shavuot* (i.e., Pentecost) sacrifices and ends with mass baptism (Acts 2). After Pentecost, Peter and John go to the temple at the hour of prayer (Acts 3:1). The first believers gathered bravely at Solomon's portico in the temple complex. And, the first apostolic healings after the resurrection were performed at the temple (Acts 5:12–16). This also serves to explain why "many of the priests became obedient to the faith" (Acts 6:7). Stephen's fatal rebuke includes a lengthy discussion as to how rejecting Moses leads to an abuse of ritual (Acts 7:35–43). Taken together, these support Klawans' conclusion, quoted above: "Jesus' followers did not separate themselves from the temple and its sacrificial worship."[12]

A theological problem caused by the inclusion of Gentiles brings the Torah and Israelite rituals to the fore of Acts in chapter 15. "What must one do to keep the Torah of Moses?" (Acts 15:5). The Torah does not appear to be on

---

whether or not he personally killed the Passover lamb is immaterial for our purposes.

12. Klawans, 217.

the verge of abrogation, but rather recontextualized for the Gentiles. The Torah, as interpreted by Jesus, now appears to point Israel outwards, rather than bring the stranger/foreigner in to perform temple rites.[13]

Notably, abuse of worship is one of the central teachings that the Torah warns against to the Gentiles (Acts 15:19). Although Peter observed that the Torah created a burden on the Jews that is unfair to place onto the Gentiles, no negative sense of the Torah-obedience bleeds through (Acts 15:10). The commendation to the Gentiles could be just as easily interpreted as a *freedom to* this practical understanding of Torah, rather than a *freedom from* Torah rites. Either way, Gentiles still must have a cognizance of their personal practices in keeping with the Jerusalem council's decision—maintaining the sexual ethos of torah and abstaining from abuse of rituals, which implies proper use.

Moreover in Acts, Paul partook in the ritual of Nazarite vows specifically for the sake of settling rumors that he was instructing Jews to "forsake Moses, telling them not to circumcise their children or walk according to our customs" (Acts 21:21). Paul agrees to practice the Nazarite vow with four others at the temple in order to confirm that he was not forsaking the Torah or its rites (Acts 21:26). While many will debate the theological significance of the scene, we only need to observe that Paul sees no deficit in practicing sacrificial rites *in the temple*. As well, Luke portrays Paul's actions directly with no critique.

Hebrews and Rituals

Finally, the Epistle to the Hebrews marks the most natural case for ritual and knowing amongst Jews. If ritual is necessary in order to know, then the epistle renowned for

13. E.g., Exod 12:48–49; Lev 18:26.

interpreting Levitical ritual to the church ought to reveal the same impetus. Building up to Hebrews 11:1, one of the more widely known epistemological statements in Christian Scripture, the author sews the language of assuredness, hope, and belief into the rhetoric of the letter. "Now *trusting belief* is the *foundational confidence* of those things for which we *hopefully expect*, the *testing* of the not-seen-things" (Heb 11:1).

However, we cannot miss that the author of Hebrews roots the reason for that assuredness, hope, and trusting belief in the history of Israel *through participation in her rituals.* In fact, Israel's rituals act as the presumed background to discerning the death of Jesus as a type of Levitical sacrifice (Heb 10)—something not entirely obvious without interpretation. In short, the logic of the appeals to Jews in Hebrews relies heavily on personal participation in the Torah's rituals. These rites enable Jews to see accurately who Jesus is.

CONCLUSIONS

I offer here the barest evidence possible of one thing: *that the Hebrew Bible and New Testament generally portray Israelites as logically separated from knowing that which they need to know apart from their participation in its specified rituals.* This view of knowing becomes coherent to us only if we can set aside the thinking-acting dichotomy in order to see how the body functions within ritual in order to see what is being shown.

In the coming chapter, we will see that rituals pervade the scientific enterprise as much any other endeavor to know. Thus, appealing to embodied ritual as central to epistemology does not denigrate biblical knowing to some religious realm of revelation. Rather, it puts biblical knowing on par with what good knowing has looked like in contemporary society.

FOR DISCUSSION

1. Think about your elementary school classroom. What are some of the embodied rituals used in order that the children might come to know science, math, language, history, and more?

2. Why might it be unhelpful to attempt to decode the symbolism of Christian rituals in order to understand their meaning?

3. How has your tradition highlighted the role of the body in coming to know that which Christians need to know? Where has your tradition diminished the role of ritual in knowing?

6

BIBLICAL AND SCIENTIFIC KNOWING

Simpatico Enterprises

Science is the pursuit and application of knowledge and understanding of the natural and social world following a systematic methodology based on evidence.[1]

WHY TALK ABOUT SCIENCE in a book on biblical knowing? When it comes to a technical understanding of knowledge, most of us only had one form of training: the scientific method. For modern Westerners, learning the scientific process was probably the only time in our formal education where we really talked about how someone can know something with a high degree of confidence. Scientific inquiry always includes a formal view of knowledge because it fundamentally asks the question "How can we know about something in the world?" and just as important, "How can we be sure?" Hence, scientific inquiry is a natural candidate for discussing knowing.

1. Science Council, "What Is Science?"

Look at how the United Kingdom's Science Council defines "science" in the quote above. Notice that it's about knowing and understanding. The definition also categorizes knowledge as something pursued, acquired, and applied. According to them, knowledge is content, which the Science Council later calls data. Though we are in a culture soaked in scientific understanding, misunderstanding persists about what scientific inquiry is. Does this definition even capture what the scientific enterprise actually does?

Instead of thinking about "what science is," let us ask a slightly different question: what do scientists actually do? We are all roughly familiar with the process called scientific discovery, even if we only have a caricature of science in our minds. We understand—even if barely—that scientists observe, measure, and posit ideas about the significance of patterns they find in reality. They then attempt to validate that significance through statistical analysis, and repeat experimentation for the sake of confirmation.[2]

As I have shown in the prior chapters, the Scriptures also share a conviction regarding process with scientific inquiry: good process will naturally produce the right kind of knowing. Hence, both Scripture and scientific communities focus on honing their processes with the presumption that it will produce better knowing. Both are also aware that processes produce knowing no matter what they do. Sloppy process produces untenable knowledge, where good

2. This version of the scientific process is only viable in certain fields, so it is not indicative of what is and is not scientific. For instance, no astrophysicist can repeat the conditions of the big bang. Likewise, no anthropologists can repeat a sacrificial burial mound as an experiment. However, this does not mean that scientific process and discovery are not possible in these fields. We also do not need to concern ourselves with the logical problems of confirmation or inductive generalization. See further Hempel, "Studies in the Logic of Confirmation (I.)," 3–7.

process produces knowing with high fidelity—like the biblical sense of "true"—to the thing being studied.

Despite our familiarity with scientific ways of knowing (i.e., scientific epistemology), even scientists themselves often misunderstand the enterprise of science. In an academic conference, I once witnessed a physics professor lament openly that most of his own colleagues at the Massachusetts Institute of Technology still believed that their primary duty was to collect facts through observation. They believed that these facts would then be put together with other facts, and from the larger collection of "scientific data," they could deduce scientific knowledge of the world. By believing this, they are echoing an overly positive view of science—through enough work and computation, they will eventually figure out the nature of the cosmos.

Although philosophers of science have discredited the idea that science will eventually work out all the facts to be known, a malingering narrative about science persists that resembles those mid-twentieth-century progressivist ideals. In the West, we have the lamentable reality of being able to obtain a doctorate of philosophy (i.e., PhD) *in a scientific field* without ever having to wrestle through the philosophy that undergirds all of science. In other words, most working scientists with a PhD are not ever required to study the "Ph" upon which their "D" is based.

Thomas Kuhn famously warned that the sober history of scientific discovery tells a different story of progress, "that a discovery . . . does not simply add one more item to the population [of facts] of the scientist's world."[3]

---

3. Kuhn, *Structure of Scientific Revolutions*, 7. It sounded as if these researchers at MIT were not required to read one of their most famous members of faculty, Thomas Kuhn, who meant to chip away at such a view.

This thin view that scientists are clinical and objective collectors of facts has been in disrepute for over six decades. And yet, that image of science—a clinical exercise of one's rational faculties applied to the world—persists despite the now-classic arguments against it. I cannot survey this cultural phenomenon of the West other than to act as a sounding board for those corrective voices from the twentieth century who sought to move past such a naïve view of science.

Michael Polanyi was one such voice. A Hungarian scientist turned philosopher, he critiqued this clinical view of science by suggesting that science is not a mechanism, but *a group of skilled people that trust each other*. Science, by Polanyi's definition, is a social fabric whose collective conscience cannot be assessed by any one person. Polanyi is worth quoting at length here:

> Indeed, nobody knows more than a tiny fragment of science well enough to judge its validity and value at first hand. For the rest he has to rely on views accepted at second hand on the authority of a community of people accredited as scientists. But this accrediting depends in its turn on a complex organization. For each member of the community can judge at first hand only a small number of his fellow members, and yet eventually each is accredited by all.[4]

Additionally, the scientific enterprise is deeply human, requiring embodied passions and rules of thumb, not objective or dispassionate observers, in order to effectively proceed:

> Nobody has ever affirmed the presuppositions of science by themselves. The discoveries of science have been achieved by the passionately

4. Polanyi, *Personal Knowledge*, 163.

sustained efforts of succeeding generations of great men [and women!], who overwhelmed the whole of modern humanity by the power of their convictions.[5]

Most astonishingly, this social fabric called "science" requires extensive chains of trust to be mutually furnished and deeply imbued in order for science to work, as it were. Or in biblical language, the system is fraught with faith:

> Science will appear then as a vast system of beliefs, deeply rooted in our history and cultivated today by a specially organized part of our society [i.e., scientists]. We shall see that science is not established by the acceptance of a formula, but is part of our mental life, shared out for cultivation among many thousands of specialized scientists throughout the world, and shared receptively, at second hand, by many millions.[6]

In what follows, I will substantiate the bold claims above. The enterprise of science *seeks to form the novice scientist into a discoverer through social and ritual practices.* I am not attempting to describe knowing in the best of circumstances, nor do I want to appeal to truth untainted by human bodies and reason. I want to sketch out a description of how a novice scientist actually gains the skill that disposes her to see the world differently than you or me. In other words, what processes and rituals enable a biologist to *just see* something at the bottom of the microscope that I can see but not perceive?

5. Ibid., 171.
6. Ibid.

HOW SCIENCE REFLECTS BIBLICAL KNOWING

Here is my boldest claim: the way scientists can know something confidently makes multiple points of contact with the biblical model of knowing. To show how this might be true, we can use the simple acronym CAARRD (say it like a pirate!): Community, Authority, Authentication, Ritual, Recognition, and Discernment. Below, I can only discuss these facets of the scientific enterprise in the broadest of ways. If one wants specific ways in which these reflect scientific knowing, Michael Polanyi's opus called *Personal Knowing* goes into exhaustive detail.

Community: Do You See What I See?

Scientists are not independent researchers; they work in community. Indeed, if a scientist claimed to prove a theory apart from peer-reviewed journals and academic societies, the community would rise to ensure that it not be viewed as fact. To be clear, an individual might produce compelling evidence that needs to be investigated further. However, for something to qualify as "scientific" knowledge, by definition it must undergo scrutiny and verification *in the community*.

How does the community verify? As skilled interpreters, they perform the same experiments in multiple locations. But even repeating the experiment itself does not support the theory. Confirmation is not even possible until two scientists actually speak to each other as colleagues. In that community, the scientists must trust each other, be sober and honest with each other, and ask each other, "Do you see what I see?" Polanyi identifies this as "conviviality," a lively college of inquiry—college being a community of colleagues.

> Articulate systems which foster and satisfy an
> intellectual passion can survive only with the

> support of a society which respects the values
> affirmed by these passions, and a society has a
> cultural life only to the extent to which it ac-
> knowledges and fulfils the obligation to lend its
> support to the cultivation of these passions.[7]

Passions do not necessarily distort the scientist's understanding; they are part and parcel of the scientist's skilled sight. As an impassioned and skilled "seer" with similar experiences and a community to which she submits, a biologist is first and foremost a colleague in a college. She and her knowing belong to a society of skilled knowers and this foundational aspect of scientific inquiry cannot be overemphasized.

The connections to biblical texts are fairly direct here. Though the great Western plague of individualism rules our day, Christians are persons in communion with both God and church. Presumably, Christians have shared experiences of God, which are weighed against Scripture and tradition. But viewing the church as a college also brings another benefit, confirmation and correction. The individuals can ask the community, "Do you see what I see?" Or, "Are you experiencing the kingdom of God like I am?"

Peter certainly approaches his experience of Gentile conversion in this way. After the Holy Spirit fell upon the house of Cornelius, a Roman centurion (Acts 10:44–48), Peter returns to his community of apostles in order to make sense of what he experienced (Acts 11:1–18). The wisdom of the apostolic community affirmed: "Then to the Gentiles also God has granted repentance that leads to life" (Acts 11:18). Like the scientist, individual experiences are not sufficient to confidently understand the experience. Confirmation and the best interpretation of experience come through the wisdom of the community, not the individual.

7. Polanyi, *Personal Knowledge*, 203.

Authority: Knowers Who Can Guide Others to Know

Though a community, not everyone in the scientific community holds equal status. As a biology student comes to know how cells reproduce, she relies upon the discernment of her professors. Senior researchers can see flaws in experiment design—from experience—not noticed by a junior colleague. In coming to know as a scientist, the skilled insights are maintained by some in the community (e.g., professors, mentors, proctors, etc.), but not all. Thus, scientific inquiry not only relies on community, but tradition within the community cultivated by the more discerning knowers.

No matter how egalitarian we want the distribution of knowledge to be, some people are more authoritative than others. By saying that traditions are cultivated, I mean that those who have the skill—for instance, the ability to spot genetic mutation in a cell—must commit to investing it in those who do not yet have the skill to see.

Of course, possessing authoritative knowledge does not mean that novices should listen to that person. The opening story of Scripture warns us about a serpent who knew truly what would happen when the couple ate the fruit. Despite his accurate knowledge of the scene, his authoritative understanding should not have been heeded according to the logic of the story. Since authority is not sufficient in Scripture to guide others, we must turn our attention to authentication.

Authentication: Credentials of Authorities

How does a novice decide which authority they will listen to? As with all enterprises of knowing, fields of science have formal and informal gatekeepers. Those gatekeepers must authenticate those to whom we should listen. Indeed, basic credentials are always needed in order to participate in the scientific community. In experimental science, these authentication processes range from terminal university degrees (e.g., PhD) to letters of recommendation from other colleagues to the number of articles published in peer-reviewed journals. Notice that all means of authentication always connect directly to the structure of the community. But no one denies that in order to teach others the required skills of one's scientific tradition, one must be specially credentialed.

In Scripture, the matter of credentials takes center stage. Again, everything the serpent says in Eden is true to the story, even if in a convoluted way. Yet, the serpent lacks authentication. He is not credentialed and therefore should not be heeded. It also explains why Scripture spends so much energy on confirming Moses' authentication as prophet, and Jesus' too. They were not only authorities that could guide Israel to know, but God also felt it necessary to comprehensively authenticate prophets such as Moses and Jesus to Israel. Before moving on, it's worth saying that scientific and biblical authentication differ most extraordinarily on this front. For prophets, authentication comes through extraordinary signs and wonders, but also through a prophet's ordinary ability to properly contextualize the Torah to a current circumstance. For the scientist, authentication comes through the ordinary means mentioned above.

Ritual: Prescribed and Embodied Acts

In order to see bone growth, tensile stress, or gamma radiation bursts, one must be trained to see. The medical doctor and I stare at the same X-ray, but she obviously sees entire worlds of things that I cannot see. If I want to *see* in the X-ray what my doctor sees, then I must embody a ritual meant to dispose me to see. But, which ritual?

The necessity of authority and authentication now come to the fore. If I want to know how to see, I must find those who are credentialed to train me (e.g., a radiology professor). In doing so, that authority will prescribe a series of embodied rituals—looking at many X-rays while having them explained to me, looking down a microscope, memorizing and drawing anatomy, etc. Herein lies the key to all such knowing. The logical gap between my seeing and not seeing a collapsed lung on a chest X-ray, for instance, can only be bridged by submitting to my authoritative instructor *and* embodying her prescribed rituals of learning. The degree to which I acknowledge the authority of the instructor and do what she says directly relates to my ability to see.

I am calling these learning practices "rituals," because they fit the prior description that I borrowed from ritual theory. If you remember, rituals are normal human practices strategically used to achieve a particular outcome. In the case of reading X-rays or discerning cell wall structures through a microscope, "looking" acts as the embodied ritual because it's not ordinary looking. Studying an X-ray acts as strategic "looking" under the guidance of an authoritative "looker," a radiologist. By both looking and being prompted by the instructor—"Do you see what I am talking about here?"—one comes to recognize that which was there the whole time, but previously unseen.

Even in research science, articles are written to other colleagues with the same basic principle. These reports describe the experiment's method—the prescribed ritual to embody—which any other scientist could presumably mimic in order to see the same results. Essentially, a scientific research article is a community-formalized ritual for colleagues to ask each other, "Do you see what I see?"

To know by means of ritual requires putting one's body through the prescribed paces in order to see what is being shown. As I demonstrated in the prior chapter, the biblical authors strike us as acutely aware of knowing in this way. Whatever the biblical rituals might do, the Scriptures present them as being epistemological: so that Israel might know. Thinking about the rituals in the church today as epistemological might force different questions than the traditional problems of interpreting the symbolism of the Eucharist, for example. Instead of focusing on the metaphysical nature of Christ's presence in bread and wine, we might need to ask, "What are we meant to know by drinking this wine and eating this bread together, and in this way?"

Recognition & Discernment: Bridging the Gap

The scientific enterprise promotes a keen sensibility for the difference between recognition and discernment. By these terms, I mean that merely recognizing some pattern in reality differs from discerning its broader implications. An example might help here.

Around 1841, Ignaz Semmelweis first *recognized* a connection between doctors working in the morgue and the death rate of new mothers in the maternity ward upstairs. As it turned out, the medical students worked on cadavers and then went up to work in the maternity ward *without ever washing their hands*. At this point in history, there was no concept of invisible microscopic creatures, later called "germs," spreading disease through contact.

Semmelweis was the first to recognize the connection. I used the word *recognize* with care because, though he saw a pattern to the deaths, he had not yet *discerned* the deaths within a theory of germs. In this sense, recognition lives on one end of a continuum with discernment on the other end.

Similarly, a medical student must first recognize a collapsed lung on an X-ray before she can genuinely discern collapsed lungs in other X-rays. One experimenter may recognize a pattern in a single experiment, but not discern its significance. Of course, researchers come into experiments with theoretical constructs already in place. Or, as philosophers of science have said, "all data is theory laden." But when the results do not fit the theory, recognizing the pattern and discerning its importance becomes a pressing task for the researcher.

After repeatedly *recognizing* a pattern, scientists will then begin to *discern* what compels the pattern to exist. Thus, *recognizing* some pattern in reality and *discerning* its significance are two different qualities of knowing. And importantly for Polanyi, discerning significance lies at the heart of scientific inquiry: "Such acts of personal judgment form an essential part of science."[8]

The biblical literature makes a similar distinction, using different language: knowing and wisdom. While everyone could see or know that YHWH opened the Red Sea to save Israel and devour Egypt (Exod 14), clearly not everyone was wise as to *why* YHWH did this (cf. Exod 32). Any Israelite could see or know that YHWH made Israel to live in booths as they wandered, but Sukkot (Feast of Booths) requires Israel to discern the grander significance of booth-living and wandering by embodying the ritual. Likewise, knowing that Jesus' body and blood were sacrificed for the new covenant does not necessarily cause one to grasp its significance. Recognizing is the first step, but wisdom appears to root itself in persistent and submitted struggle to discern the transcendent patterns of life: how pornography dehumanizes, when a community fails at humility, why rhythms in life provide stability, etc. The wisdom to understand such complex affairs cannot be found alone or in one instance. They require cultivated communities that

---

8. Polanyi, *Personal Knowledge*, 20.

are persistently attentive to the guidance of Scripture and that soberly look at reality.

CONCLUSIONS

Though much of what I have said above lines up with the theology of T. F. Torrance and others, few have made the direct link between what the Scriptures are doing with knowledge in reference to the scientific enterprise.[9] It is rather surprising to find out that these ancient Semites describe a pattern of reasoned knowing that so aptly fits with modern scientific inquiry. Belonging to a community, establishing trust worthy of authentication, and practicing rites meant to bring about authoritative knowing all function to help novices first *recognize* and later *discern* patterns in the real world. This process of knowing guides Israelites truly according to their own accounts and still guides the scientific enterprise truly today.

9. For those familiar with the work of T. F. Torrance, it will be obvious to some that I am not arguing for anything drastically different from Torrance's theological utilization of Polanyi's scientific epistemology. Torrance sought to show that "the task and problems of a scientific theology are not very different from" a properly understood scientific epistemology. Torrance, *Theology and Scientific Culture*, 161. Torrance showed the affinity that theology and science share in their desire to know and processes that made knowing work well. This present work is only unique in that I contend that biblical texts themselves share affinity with what Torrance and others have argued for regarding Polanyi's view of scientific knowing. Of course, this is not a claim I can defend here. But I am not alone in seeing these affinities. Cf. Gunton, "Truth of Christology"; "Knowledge and Culture"; Hart, *Faith Thinking*. Although Polkinghorne regularly appeals to Polanyi, he only does so regarding the more individualistic and responsible rationalizing aspects of *Personal Knowledge*. Polkinghorne, *Theology in the Context of Science*, 73–75.

FOR DISCUSSION

1. What do people mean when they say that something is a scientific fact?

2. How do Christians in your Church faithfully submit themselves and their own religious experiences to the wisdom of the community?

3. How does your Christian community control for poor interpretation of Scripture in the lives of its members?

4. Who are the authoritative guides and how is their authentication established within your Christian community?

7

PRACTICAL IMPLICATIONS OF BIBLICAL KNOWING

The Discerning Church

THIS PENULTIMATE CHAPTER IS a bit longer than the others because I want to explore how this works out in the daily lives of families, churches, and other organizations.

I want to strongly suggest that our theology, the way in which we live out what we know, must be reconciled to the view of knowing described in the Scriptures.[1] By that, I mean that theology has often considered matters in terms of *knowing what God knows*. Intentionally or not, I too often ask myself the question: what does God know about this? However, I am not sure that is always or often the correct question to ask.

What then should we seek? Instead of attempting to pick the mind of God, the Scriptures seem to consistently direct us *to see what the prophets are trying to show us*. It's

---

1. This chapter is adapted (with additional material) from Dru Johnson, *Biblical Knowing*, ch. 9.

akin to taking a class in order to know what the professor knows rather than to develop the skill of seeing what the professor is showing me. First, what a professor teaches in class is often done through rituals of education not intended to transfer her knowledge to my brain, a thing only possible in the fictive world of movies like *The Matrix*. Second, if the professor is a subject matter expert, the course content looks different to her than to me. I am only getting a slice of *what she knows* and when she looks at those same slices, she has a richer and more nuanced grasp of them. I defeat the purpose behind the classroom rituals (e.g., dialogue, lecture, memorizing, quizzing, rhetorical question-asking, etc.) by attempting to *know what she knows*.

What did the prophets see? Although the prophets are always trying to show Israel what they themselves should see (they were first called "seers" before the title "prophet"), the prophets most often call Israel to recontextualize the Torah's teaching for their present circumstances. The Torah was a deep well of wisdom to which the prophets regularly returned in order to guide Israel. In order to see what the prophets are showing Israel, a Torah-formed life is the prerequisite.

But merely seeing is not enough. Israelites saw the wonders in Egypt, yet some still recognized the golden calf as Israel's savior (Exodus 32). Though ten lepers were healed in Luke's gospel, nine of them do not appear to discern the significance of that healing (Luke 17:9). Knowing well means that beyond mere recognition, we can integrate one event into a grander vision. In Scripture, this is called wisdom or discernment. Discernment requires constantly looking and re-looking at reality under the instruction of the Torah and the prophets, including Jesus and the apostles. Deuteronomy reports that living under the instruction of the Torah in this way "will be your wisdom and your understanding in the sight of the peoples" (Deut 4:6).

KNOWING AS A ROLE OF THE CHURCH

Below, I will think out loud about some aspects of biblical knowing that directly help (or hinder) the work of the church. Thinking about the church as a community of knowers—people on various ventures of knowing—can offer different questions and challenge what we emphasize in matters of community, worship, and service.

Seeing Beyond the Surface

The bond that ties together what the Bible calls *the prophets* and *the wise* is their ability to see beyond the superficial symptoms down to the heart of the matter. The wise see beyond the symptoms to the pattern from which the symptoms emerge. This type of seeing grasps that a child's fever is a superficial feature of the influenza virus, for example. Anyone who has been around Christian culture is certainly familiar with "false righteousness," where a person's behavior and motivations do not match. Pastors can tell you about that sweet woman who spews venom and rage if you change the color of the church's carpet. They certainly would know the gentle and modest man who wields totalitarian control over his family behind the closed doors of his home. Upon looking at the surface of their lives, everything looks great. But the truth is, churchgoers can often be surprised to find out who is physically abusing their spouse or habitually visiting prostitutes.

Conversely, we have all seen those families or children who were so wrecked by violence or tragedy that we could not conceive of anything good coming out of it. Cultures of luxury and poverty can breed all the wrong sentiments about what it means to be human. We see children who behave so heinously that we honestly question if they themselves are irredeemably evil. We know families that are so shattered by wealth, abuse, or poverty that our imaginations do not run wild enough to muster hope for their futures. Just consider what it would be like to have King David as a father, or even worse, as a husband!

Despite all this, we see the prophets of Israel, including Jesus, regularly indicting those who look good on the surface. We hear their words of hope to the desperately poor and wrecked families among them. The prophets see beyond the surface. They see a kingdom arising from the impenetrable logic of Jesus' public teaching and actions. They see the twisted wreckage right under the surface of public righteousness. They see hope for the exploited and the exploiters like King David, whom we might consider incorrigible or "damaged goods."

Consider this: *if the Scriptures teach that knowing well requires apprenticeship, then our ability to see beyond the presenting symptoms of life is proportional to the degree that we submit to our trainer's instruction.*

As an example, I used to work as a pastor in a suburban and predominately white American community. We wanted to serve "the poor" around us, but we really did not know how. We convened a group to discuss and pray about this problem and eventually decided that we needed guidance. After hunting around a bit, we ended up apprenticing with an urban church who had been working with international refugees for years. Only after spending quality time under their tutelage did we realize how much training we needed. We would go to help new immigrants and just did not know where to start. We did not know what they needed. The immigrants usually did not speak English. So, they could not guide us either.

When our coaches from the urban church would come into those same houses with us, they could quickly ask a few questions from the families and then explain to us how we could best serve these people. This was great. It made a night and day difference. However, we had to ask the coaching church to explain to us the clues that allowed them to see through this impenetrable surface. Without having the coaches explain the clues, their coaching would have been more like giving us a fish than teaching us how to fish. By that coaching, we learned how to discern what service looked like in these refugee micro-communities in the American Midwest.

One more example: Working with children, it's not unusual to see shocking behaviors, even expressed by small children. One can view the child as a *bad kid*, but more than likely, that kid does not know why they are acting this way either. Labeling the child a *bad kid* only addresses the surface of her life, the presenting symptoms. Of course, a coach can bring expert guidance and show us how to look beyond the behavior and start looking for different clues that might be the source of the behavior such as Post Traumatic Stress or Attachment Reactive Disorder.

If we see our service and worship as a venture in knowing, an inquiry, we will be compelled to stop being satisfied with the surface features, whether they are socially acceptable or not. We will look for the pattern below the surface. This is basically what I mean when I claim that we ought to have a sober view on reality. I am arguing that merely inspecting peoples' righteous or reprehensible behaviors is insufficient for knowing them, or knowing cats even, or anything at all. If we do not actually know people, then we cannot encourage, respect, or correct them apart from pretentious platitudes.

Offering Real Wisdom to the Church

I have heard it said that all claims are claimed claims. In other words, when I say that the moon is full tonight, *I* am personally claiming *that I* have real access to reality outside of myself. When we make claims about the world and its residents, we are inherently offering guidance. There is no neutral ground when making claims. The colloquial lie, "I'm just sayin'" taps into this sensibility where we want to make a claim and still seem neutral (e.g., "He never did pay you back the loan. I'm just sayin'.").

On the flip side, there is no neutral position where independent humans learn completely unguided. Because our convictions make claims and we learn from the claims of others, we must be aware of the voices operative over us, and even more, how our voice guides others.

If authoritative voices inherently govern how we know the world, then recognizing who stands in that position of authority becomes a chief concern for the church. Even more, recognizing who ought to stand in the position of guide is of ultimate consequence. For Christians, the relationship between Scripture and us must be meted out upon this boundary. For many of us, the Scriptures are the prophetic voice, quite literally an assembly of the prophets' voices. They have the ultimate position as prophet over the church and her disciples, the voice that trumps all other voices. This does not mean that we can simply assert that the Scriptures guide us plainly in all circumstances.[2] We all read the Bible through the lenses of our churches and experiences—our traditions.

2. None have escaped the postmodern critique that showed all reading of the text is interpretation, bound up in our cultures, traditions, communities, and personalities. Hence, we must acknowledge the cultural baggage that we bring to our reading of the Scriptures that helps and hinders us.

The question of authoritative voice is really a question of our goal: what is it that we seek to know by means of this person's authoritative guidance? Trevor Hart puts it to us most pointedly when he says:

> The pertinent question, the decision which we have to make, is not *whether* we will submit to such voices, but rather *which* voices we will submit to, and at what points and under what conditions shall we feel able or obliged to challenge what they are saying to us.[3]

As leaders in the church, we also need to consider with sobriety how we act as that voice to those around us. Moreover, do we seek to point people to a plurality of voices including Scripture, or just our own voice? And, how do we handle challenges to our authority?

Knowing How to Instruct Each Other

It will come as no surprise that the implications for biblical knowing in the church might not be radically different from the way many churches already operate. The catholic church—universal and throughout history—remains one gigantic organization directed to be a venture in knowing.[4] How does biblical knowing inform our view of teaching, counseling, and discipleship, all of which are epistemological acts? I can only make suggestions, but here are a few.

Teaching

The question of knowing for the teacher or preacher ought to take center stage: What must be established first in order

---

3. Hart, *Faith Thinking*, 177.

4. The term "catholic," meaning "universal," is not to be confused with the Roman Catholic Church.

to bring others to know?[5] From the priorities found in Scripture, the primacy of our authentication as teachers supersedes all else. Notice that I did not claim that authoritative knowledge was supreme, although a teacher ought to know the Scriptures and life both soberly and authoritatively. However, without authentication, there is no bond between the teacher and the apprentice that can enable knowing. Without mutual commitment to the process, no genuine effort can make knowing happen.

Authentication is caught best by the well-worn phrase, "earning the right to be heard." After all, no one wants to expend effort under the apprenticeship of someone who may or may not guide us to know correctly. Authoritative knowledge then usually takes second chair to authentication in teaching and preaching.

Sometimes, authority does act as authentication. When Jesus calms the sea and winds, his authority over creation helps to authenticate him. If someone claimed that she had a black belt in martial arts, seeing her perform the art could help to authenticate her. But again, the demonstrated ability helps to authenticate, but it is not the only mark of authentication. Unbelievably, even Jesus' Father eventually had to get involved in Jesus' authentication, coming down on a mountain and compelling the disciples, "Listen to him" (Mark 9:7).

The most effective teaching establishes credibility for the authoritative teacher. It also requires the teacher and learner to be fully committed to each other and to the process. Some authorities are better guides. Some are more

5. When addressing teaching I am including preaching into the category. I know that many have made distinctions about their differences, but when a person guides a group to see something that they could not previously see, then the epistemological process is at work. Whether or why we would call it either "teaching" or "preaching" is a slightly different matter that I do not intend to take up here.

committed to the process, but not so committed to the learner. But in order to develop the skill to know something well, we must have reasons to commit to the process. Hence, authentication is not merely a badge worn by teachers, but the evidence of their obligated commitment to teaching. Further, authentication includes the learner's sense that she will actually come to know something, to develop a skill of discernment. Thus, knowing requires both hope and trust that this process will work.

The trio of trust, hope, and love fit nicely here in the category of authentication. I am not importing Paul's discussion into mine (1 Cor 13:13), but noticing that without reasons to trust the authority (faith), an expectation that a discernible skill will result (hope), and the commitment of both parties to each other and the process (love), knowing is staved off or out of sorts with reality.

Teachers and preachers submit to a biblical process of knowing when they attend to their authentication. Good teachers understand the reasons why they can be trusted and mistrusted. Such teachers cultivate those reasons to earn trust much like God himself does with his own people throughout the Hebrew Bible and New Testament. Relational stability, awareness of our own historical environs, vulnerability to be wrong, compassion, and the ability to commit are just some factors that enliven our authentication among those we hope to teach. Brute appeals to power or authority should deflate any novice knower's confidence. If God has created humanity to know in community, and Jesus' life exhibits that mission *par excellence*, then the biblical ethic anticipates and expects that we will cultivate habits of authenticity.

As a practical example, I have found that when I am new to a group of students or parishioners, it is often better to teach in a way where I am showing my work, so to speak.

I attempt to teach expositionally so that my students can see for themselves the fidelity of my teaching to the Scriptures. In the church, this might mean that a new pastor would preach with more exegetical transparence and avoid heavily topical or theological sermons for the first year or so.

Submitting to Reality

I have intentionally held at bay the discussion regarding non-persons as authorities, mainly because Scripture very rarely employs it. I could make the case that wisdom litera-ture and parables often employ nonpersonal reality as an authority. The Proverbs use the ant as an authority on the wisdom of work (6:6). Jesus uses seeds and trees to instruct us about the nature of the kingdom of God (Mark 4:30–32). But even in those cases, it is the voice of a person direct-ing us to reflect on those concrete realities that brings us to know.

Paul claims in Romans 1 that all of creation brings us to awareness of God (*sensus divinitatis*). However, the qual-ity of that knowing does not seem to act as an authoritative guide in the process of knowing God himself. Rather, cre-ation is in a supporting role to the Holy Spirit, which brings us to know God.

Considering the ways in which reality can guide us has merit, for there are direct implications for our preaching and teaching. Namely, we want to ensure that the process of knowing—especially in the church—does not solely focus on knowing God, but also knowing the real world. More specifically, objective reality keeps us sober about what we might and can know. For if our preaching is bent on some other heavenly world, something that cannot be corrected or guided by reality, then we give up our ability to let real-ity guide and shape us. And as I have tried to show in this work, God is intent on using creation and his recognizable acts in creation to bring Israel to specific knowledge.

Even more than supporting roles, there are also direct ways in which objective reality acts as our authoritative guide if we submit to its way of guiding us. If we want to know the historical context of a rock in our garden, how could the rock itself guide us? We could pretend to be an authority over the rock, threatening it with a hammer and demand that it tell us what kind of a rock it is (e.g., sedentary, ultramafic, ore, glass, etc.) and how long it has been in the place we found it. Obviously, this is an absurd example. After all, why would a rock know our classifications for minerals? And, it is also absurd because rocks do not speak, at least not directly. There are ways to discern what kind of a rock it is, according to the classifications that we have constructed, and even ways to discern its age and conditions of its geological origins. But we must submit to the rock's way of speaking to us. We must understand that rocks cannot authenticate their age or lineage by means of a driver's license.

And so we can come to know something about a rock, but not by asking absurd questions. Rather, we can begin a properly contextualized process of knowing only when we are willing to ask the question: How can this rock tell us about itself? Similarly, I've been told that wild horses work much the same way. When captured, *they* will only let us know *them* after we enter *their* world on *their* terms. *They* become the authority on how we will know them, revealing only their ability to be sweet after we have spent the right amount of time with them, learned to lower our voice, monitor our eye movements, and so on. It has been observed that children (and humans of other ages!) work in a very similar fashion, being the authority on how they will reveal themselves to us. When we are too aggressive, or ask absurd questions, then people will often close down, defend, hibernate from us, and no longer guide us to know the more vulnerable version of them.

Learning how to properly submit to creation in order to know it is also instructive for our treatment of Scripture. First, learning how creation reveals itself to us helps us ground our preaching and teaching in reality. The real world is not accidental to God's kingdom that has already come and is coming. And so understanding our real world and groping toward our Maker by what has been made should not be accidental to our preaching. Second, we learn how to know God in Scripture by practicing on creation, by learning how to ask the right questions, and by learning to eject or modify the absurd questions.

How does creation gain authentication with us? In all these instances—the objective reality of a rock in the world, a live animal thrashing, or even a foster child entering a new family—the reality of these people and things being present in the world authenticates them to us. The brute reality of events and objects, before we even get to the interpretation of these things, self-authenticates them to us as real. An example would be helpful.

The objective reality of YHWH as the pillar of fire, a baby in Mary's womb, Jesus' public miracles, the resurrection, the Holy Spirit poured out on the Gentiles, and more are all meant to function as revelation (i.e., revealing something about God and his covenants) precisely because they were objectively real events. These nonpersonal realities—events said to happen in the real world despite how anyone would interpret them—confronted those Israelites and had to be understood or denied.[6] They were authorita-

6. Pregnancy and resurrection are nonpersonal only in that they are a real situation that obliges response, despite the fact that they involve persons in both cases.

tive inasmuch as they were objectively real, recognizable (i.e., not secret), and demanding that the participants in those stories no longer view themselves as authorities. The infant in Mary's womb meant that she was no longer able to demand answers to absurd questions. Reality now demands questions from her.

In the same vein, the scientist submits to nonpersonal reality. Her questions are posed and modified in the process of research precisely because the reality being studied is an authority on the study. The reality of molecular structures or animal behavior modifies her questions, rejects absurdities, and is authenticated to the scientist because it is presumed to be objectively real.

If this is even partially correct, the implications spill directly into teaching and preaching. Any authority who attempts to guide others to know risks being de-authenticated when she extends knowing beyond reality. Or, at the very least, the teacher must let reality sober and temper her knowledge. Seeking to explain the essences of the heavens or realities of which she has not personally understood can discredit the teacher. What she espouses must respect the real world, and in some fundamental way, submit to its authority. It cannot be Platonic in the improper sense that it cannot suppose that the heavens are the true reality and the material world is the source of our deception. Our theology cannot be what Nietzsche regularly called "world-fleeing," seeing our bodies as the prison of a soul that seeks the seduction of escape to the heavens.[7] Authentic teaching jives with reality because it respects both the creation by YHWH

---

7. "It was the sick and decaying who despised body and earth and invented the heavenly realm and the redemptive drops of blood . . . . Ungrateful, these people deemed themselves transported from their bodies and this earth." Nietzsche, *Thus Spoke Zarathustra*, 144–45.

and the image of God in humanity that can see beyond a broken reality, marred by sinners sinning in sinfulness.

IDENTIFYING ABSURD QUESTIONS

I teach many freshmen courses and have noticed that well-intentioned students often bring the wrong questions to the conversation. The trick is to teach them how to ask better questions, which is usually a result of listening carefully to Scripture for a long time. Initially, they often ask questions like, "Is it a sin to do X according to the Bible?" We ultimately end up re-forming that question to:

Is it wise to do X?

How is X discussed in Scripture?

What are images like X in Scripture that can guide my thinking?

Those initial questions we ask are not wrong, but the normal tentative probings that help us listen to the biblical texts. However, those questions can become absurd when the questioner refuses to give them up. When we place the Bible on trial, act as the prosecutor, ask binary questions, and demand crisp answers to our malformed ideas. We may demand:

Is it or is it not true that sex before marriage is a sin?

Smoking is morally neutral?

Procreation is an individual choice of couples?

We need to help them identify that disposition and kind of question as absurd, giving reasons for why it betrays the wrong ethic of knowing.

Even our theological questions themselves must be circumscribed by reality. There are some theological questions, even big questions, which run the risk of being epistemologically absurd. The Scriptures and reality itself might preclude us from pursuing them. Even the question, "What *is* God?" might not turn out to be a helpful question, depending on what is meant by it. Since, if God is like the rock, mustang, or child discussed above, then the manner in which he has chosen to reveal himself is instructive and possibly restrictive for what can be known about him.

For instance, we all agree that certain medical experiments, while they might provide very useful understanding, would be inappropriate to pursue. If we can agree that it is absurd to film how long it takes human infants to die without any human touch (a real research question at one point in history!), then we already believe that there is an ethical aspect to all inquiries. Thus, pursuits in knowing are fundamentally ethical in that some things that can be known should not be known.

The matter of what questions are then unethical or absurd must be reconciled by some understanding of Scripture's ethical teaching. In other words, it seems that Scripture has already fixed an ethic generally within humanity and specifically in the church that restricts our pursuits. Our common conviction is that medical research requiring cruel human death, even though it may lead to a profound insight, would actually lead us away from understanding what it is to be a human in covenant with God. That line of research takes us away from the very thing we are trying to understand under the auspices of gaining more knowledge. As Nietzsche expressed it in his zeal to attack some philosophers of his day:

> They think they are honoring a thing if they de-historicize it, . . . if they make a mummy out of it. Everything that philosophers have handled, for thousands of years now, has been a conceptual mummy; nothing real escaped their hands alive.[8]

8. Nietzsche, *Twilight of the Idols*, 18.

Thus, those who teach must be very careful to understand what kinds of pursuits are at stake. Further, good teaching requires the skill of identifying bad questions, ones that inherently deceive us into believing that we know more and more through less and less covenantal constraints.

EARNING THE RIGHT TO BE HEARD

Further, those who preach and teach must work to reaffirm their authentication. Ordination and university degrees do not imbue accreditation by fiat or magic. Ordination and theological training are merely entryways that have, hopefully, already shaped the teacher along the way. Accreditation comes by fidelity to a call, which I would contend must be accredited through the church. Even more, faithfulness to reality entails loving the broken world, the learner, and the process of knowing enough to faithfully participate. We must earn the right to be heard because we have been transformed in our discernment of the kingdom of God in its particulars. The impetus to teach and preach under the sway of our own transformed view must be tested for its mettle and trueness to reality by accrediting agencies (e.g., denominational bodies, churches, etc.). For the teacher, authenticity must be meted out with a willingness to let accreditation be established and reestablished every so often.[9] If the life of King Solomon teaches us nothing else, discernment is a skill that can be lost and so it demands periodic reaccreditation.

Finally, because the authority of pastors and teachers requires authentication, teachers earn the right to be heard by enacting the Scriptures outside of the time of teaching. By living the teaching of Scripture, they gain authentication

9. This is why I hesitate at the title "preacher," as it is a foreign term in post-Christian societies such as the United Kingdom and runs the risk of presuming authentication with the title itself.

to teach others when they hone their skilled knowledge outside the sermon or class. This requires regular evaluation of their ability to discern how the kingdom of God operates in new circumstances. Skills are honed and can be lost. Good knowing requires checks and balances to ensure that the skill is still accreditable. If I were to be dogmatic, teachers who do not submit themselves to the most basic requirements of discipleship cannot be accredited.

Discipleship and Counseling

The primary difference between the epistemological process in preaching and counseling is the public versus private nature of the processes. Although good preaching and teaching is a dialogue to some extent, it has most often been modeled as monologue. Nevertheless, how is counseling a private dialogue framed toward knowing? What is meant to be known and how?

Many young pastors are shocked—I know that I was— when people begin to reveal extremely desperate situations to us, which often require intense counseling. We are in no way prepared for this from seminary training alone. The skill of counseling is the ability to see patterns emerge from the chaotic mess that the counselee self-reports to us. Complicating matters, the self-report is often inaccurate or misleading. The visionary wisdom of the counselor notices one pattern among many. But beyond noticing a pattern, the skilled wisdom enables her to work out a process through which the counselee will come to know for herself the reality within which they struggle. There can be many other facets of life mitigating the process of counseling: church discipline, family systems, identity confusion, abuse, addiction, etc. But discernment is the consummate ability required of the counselor. The counseling process, like teaching, requires Paul's trio of trust, hope, and love in order for both parties to know well.

If humans are created for covenantal relationship with God and others, then shattered families and individual relationships require a significant amount of savvy in order to understand what is central versus peripheral. Indeed, all counselors will tell about the failure of counselees to commit to the process of knowing for reasons of trust, lack of hope that it will change anything, or failure to feel loved.

Counseling, discipleship, and even the application portion of preaching all share this in common: humans need someone outside of themselves to guide them. Indeed, this was normal before the Fall (Gen 3). The man was "not good" when it was just YHWH Elohim and him in the garden. The man needed both someone else (God) and reality itself (the animals) to lead him to see who his proper mate would be. With broken humanity, we desperately need others so that we can come to know who we are, and to know ourselves soberly.

Giving Reason to Ritual

If Israel's rituals are epistemological, then framing Christian ritual similarly marks a sensible path for churches. Rote performance has its own benefits to learning. Yet, a reflective view of rites as transformative can complement the rote performance and guard against seeing rituals as transactions.

It's no secret that many people in the church recite Scripture, pray, kneel at the altar, or bow before the bread of communion with a tinge of payoff in their minds. Consciously or not, our presumption when performing rituals can include the thought, "I am doing this thing in order to get something from God." I petition God with prayer, which implies that I ought to receive. I kneel at the altar, which means, "Okay God, I'm being very serious about this." Like an incantation that wards off bad mojo, I recite Scriptures in hard times that I think will somehow ward off the problems I am experiencing.

However, if one of the primary functions of Israelite (and Christian) ritual is to show us something we could not otherwise see, then the tit-for-tat view of rituals does not fit as easily. If I may give a crude example: students who do their coursework merely for a desired grade tend to see all the class rituals of reading, writings, and quizzing as transactional. For them, they do *the things* and the professor gives the expected grade. However, if the student and professor genuinely believe that all of those processes and rituals are meant to transform their view of the course topic, then the ritual acts become the instruments of transformation. It's not exclusively true, but under this transformational view of the classroom, the grade become the natural consequence of the performance and therefore takes a subsidiary role.

Becoming a People Prepared

Alcoholics Anonymous meetings always include sober (pun intended) and non-romantic public introductions: "Hi, I'm Dru, and I'm an alcoholic." There is little pretense as to why you are at the meeting and what you struggle with. When John the Baptist comes Elijah-like to prepare Israel for the Messiah, he offers a cleansing baptism to the Jews who were repenting of sin. However, he also welcomes the crowds by saying, "You brood of vipers! Who warned you to flee from the wrath to come" (Luke 3:7)? There is little pretense as to why Jews came there. (I remember reading the gospels for the first time as an adult convert and thinking to myself, "Wow! John the Baptist is kind of a jerk.")

As in science and all of life, failing to be sober about the real world devastates the process of knowing.

Romanticizing people, institutions, or positions in life means that what we come to know through those pre-romanced visions has no promise of being connected to the real world. Scientists wrestle endlessly with trying to strip away variables that might color or tint their view of a particular reality. Because they long to make real contact with the real world, they value a sober view, even if it is not as seductive or hopeful.

Nevertheless, reality will make course corrections for us even if we want to imbibe our romantic views of people, locations, education, occupations, status symbols, etc. One could even argue that romanticism is a form of idolatry, which makes sense of the prophets' common rebuke concerning idols, "These are not real."[10] *But reality will catch up and overtake our romanticism.* As Esther Meek puts it:

> The real world gives back, and it gives as good as it gets. How could we ever think that in knowing the knower determines reality? Try telling that to a tidal wave, or to your motion-sick stomach. Reality too often knocks us over. It might as well be saying: You treat me right and maybe, if you're lucky, I might treat you right![11]

Coming to know and doing it well means a somber, determined, and steely view of reality. But if we choose to romantically or pessimistically tint our view, reality fights back too.

EPILOGUE

Scout Finch did not discern the process of her learning to read. She could not have, because she did not remember

---

10. Cf. Deut 32:21; Jer 10:1–11; Isa 2:1–22; etc.
11. Meek, *Longing to Know*, 142.

it. She did not understand that, under her father's patient guidance, she embodied ritualized practices of reading over and over, meant to transform her vision of the print on the page from mere script to news about Maycomb County's goings-on.

Reading acts as a good illustration because merely *knowing facts* about language (e.g., what is a verb, what is an article, when do I use a semicolon, etc.) does not equate to knowing the language. Moreover, merely *knowing how* to read does not represent the skill of knowing either. Yes, reading is a skillful act, but it's more than that. Once we have been transformed into *readers*, we can never just look at the English words on a page. *We always will read them and it will feel as if we have always been able to do so.*

Knowing English also means that we can wisely assert things such as, "It's difficult to communicate your sarcastic body language in an email." We do not need to try every single grammatical and syntactical construction that describes your body language and sense of sarcasm in order to know that it will not translate well into text. We *just know* that text cannot do that. How do we know that? Because we have come to know both written language and body language, we can discern that one cannot directly translate to the other without remainder. However, we did not come to know *that* by trial and error! We discern it through our grasp of both body language and written English.

The movie *Boyhood* has been widely acclaimed in the year that I write this. Methodologically, no movie has ever done what *Boyhood*'s director did: shoot a film about children growing up with real children growing up over the course of twelve years. You actually see them mature during a 165-minute film. Cliché as it sounds, watching this happen in compressed filmic time feels surreal.

When asked about filming a movie over twelve years, Ethan Hawke (who played the boy's father in the film) spoke about the director's reason for attempting such an audacious technique. The director's explanation speaks to what Scout Finch misunderstood with her own ability to read. For Scout Finch, she did not know how to read, and then at some point in the past, she did know how to read. For her it was a single point of enlightenment. Ethan Hawke describes Richard Linklater's motivation in directing this film over twelve years:

> There's this lie in every film—even the best ones—about childhood, this little, tiny lie you have to accept that somehow, some enlightenment moment *happens in one moment, rather than being in a series of moments when we come of age.* You know, they [moments of enlightenment] may come to feel like one [moment], but [the director] was saying, wouldn't it be amazing to make a movie where we actually just captured all the little moments? The feeling of growing up could actually be tactile.[12]

Boyhood recognizes and celebrates the moments that add up to a transformed view of reality. Learning to read, grasping cell structure, discerning family systems dynamics, or measuring cosmic radiation all come in a series of graspings. Scout Finch cannot be held accountable for failing to understand the guided process of knowing; after all, she is only the voice of a nine-year-old girl.

However, Scripture holds a different standard. In the Bible, knowing is central to life in Eden, Israel's life in Canaan, and Israel's extension into the New Testament community. *Understanding how we understand* appears to be a persistent project of Israel's prophets, including Jesus and

12. Hawke and Arquette, interview by Terry Gross, italics mine.

his apostles. Further, holding up a misshapen or rosecol-ored mirror to our own process of knowing leaves us with no better understanding than that of Scout Finch (sorry Jean Louise). I have contended throughout this book that an accurate view of knowing must begin under the guidance of the prophets, compiled in Scripture, which evinces the real ways humans know today.

8

FURTHER READING

LOOKING AT THE SCRIPTURES for philosophical content is
a relatively new field of research, though not entirely new.
For instance, when Thomas Aquinas encounters Aristotle's
statement that a woman is essentially "a fetus gone awry,"
he was not afraid to put The Philosopher (aka Aristotle) in
his place about the metaphysical goodness of women. He
corrects Aristotle by using the creation account found in
Genesis.[1] In other words, he felt that the creation account
in Genesis offered a philosophical principle about creatures
that was in direct tension with Aristotle's misogynist views.
The story of creation itself, Aquinas recognized, argues for
something.

Aquinas is by no means the first or only philosopher/
theologian to see philosophical positions defended in the
teaching and stories of Scripture. However, not many in
scholarship have maintained a steady focus on examining
philosophical positions directly from Scripture. Therefore,
the contributions are scarce.

Recently, biblical scholars are finding overlap with
philosophical literature and vice versa. Jaco Gericke, Yoram

---

1. Aquinas, *Summa Theologica*, Question 92.

Hazony, and I have started a program unit in the Society of Biblical Literature called "Hebrew Bible and Philosophy." It aims to foster scholarly research in the philosophical discourse of the Hebrew Bible. Currently, there is no New Testament counterpart, but that will hopefully change.

Below, I offer a brief list of the key works in biblical studies and philosophy that attempt to make contact with the Scriptural view of knowing or Scripture's native philosophy in general. Of course, the list below does not represent the breadth of work currently published, but gives some good starting points into the literature. I will note books with academic or technical ambitions with an asterisk (*). *Above all the recommendations below, everyone should read Qohelet (Ecclesiastes), entirely and regularly.*

EPISTEMOLOGY IN BIBLICAL STUDIES

Avrahami, Yael. *Senses of Scripture: Sensory Perception in the Hebrew Bible*. New York: T. & T. Clark, 2013.*

Healy, Mary, and Robin Parry, eds. *The Bible and Epistemology*. Colorado Springs: Paternoster, 2007.

Johnson, Dru. *Biblical Knowing: A Scriptural Epistemology of Error*. Eugene, OR: Cascade, 2013.

———. *Epistemology and Biblical Theology: From the Pentateuch to the Gospel of Mark*. New York: Routledge, 2017.*

———. *Knowledge by Ritual: A Biblical Prolegomenon to Sacramental Theology*. Journal of Theological Interpretation Supplement Series. Winona Lake, IN: Eisenbrauns, 2016.*

O'Dowd, Ryan. *The Wisdom of Torah: Epistemology in Deuteronomy and the Wisdom Literature*. Göttingen: Vandenhoeck & Ruprecht, 2009.*

Scott, Ian W. *Paul's Way of Knowing: Story, Experience, and the Spirit*. Grand Rapids: Baker Academic, 2008.

CHRISTIAN EPISTEMOLOGY IN PHILOSOPHY

Meek, Esther L. *A Little Manual for Knowing*. Eugene, OR: Cascade, 2014.

———. *Loving to Know: Covenant Epistemology*. Eugene, OR: Cascade, 2011.

———. *Longing to Know: The Philosophy of Knowledge for Ordinary People*. Grand Rapids: Brazos, 2003.

Moser, Paul K. *The Elusive God: Reorienting Religious Epistemology*. New York: Cambridge University Press, 2009.

Plantinga, Alvin. *Warranted Christian Belief*. New York: Oxford University Press, 2000.[2]*

Smith, James K. A. *Imagining the Kingdom: How Worship Works*. Grand Rapids: Baker Academic, 2013.

Stump, Eleonore. *Wandering in Darkness*. New York: Oxford University Press, 2012.

APPROACHES TO BIBLICAL PHILOSOPHY

Gericke, Jaco. *The Hebrew Bible and Philosophy of Religion*. Atlanta: SBL, 2013.

Hazony, Yoram. *The Philosophy of Hebrew Scripture*. New York: Cambridge University Press, 2012.

2. While Alvin Plantinga's work is pioneering within the field of analytic epistemology, and he genuinely seeks to represent the Christian faith, I would recommend Paul Moser's or Eleonore Stump's work as suitable guide points that make better contact with Scripture from the contemporary world of philosophy. See my admiration and critique of Plantinga in *Biblical Knowing*, 173–80.

BIBLIOGRAPHY

Avrahami, Yael. *The Senses of Scripture: Sensory Perception in the Hebrew Bible*. Library of Hebrew Bible / Old Testament Studies 545. New York: T. & T. Clark, 2012.

Baker, Lynn Rudder. "Christians Should Reject Mind-Body Dualism." In *Contemporary Debates in the Philosophy of Religion*, edited by Michael L. Peterson and Raymond J. VanArragon, 327–43. Malden, MA: Blackwell, 2004.

Barth, Karl. *Church Dogmatics*. Vol. 4.2. Edited by G. W. Bromiley and T. F. Torrance. Translated by Geoffrey Bromily. Edinburgh: T. & T. Clark, 1961.

Bell, Catherine. *Ritual Theory, Ritual Practice*. New York: Oxford University Press, 2009.

Benjamint444 (Wikimedia user). *Navel orange1*. Image. Dec 25, 2008. http://commons.wikimedia.org/wiki/File:Navel_orange1.jpg.

Berg, Werner. "Der Sündenfall Abrahams und Saras nach Gen 16:1–6." *Biblische Notizen* 19 (1982) 7–14.

Bergen, Wesley. "Studying Ancient Israelite Ritual: Methodological Considerations." *Religious Compass* 1.5 (2007) 579–86.

Calvin, John. *Commentaries on the First Book of Moses, Called Genesis*. Edinburgh: Calvin Translation Society, 1847.

———. *Commentary on a Harmony of the Evangelists, Matthew, Mark and Luke* 2. Translated by William Pringle. Edinburgh: Calvin Translation Society, 1845–46.

Carasik, Michael. *Theologies of the Mind in Biblical Israel*. Oxford: Peter Lang, 2005.

Cassuto, Umberto A. *Commentary on the Book of Genesis*. Jerusalem: Magnes, 1961.

Douglas, Mary. *Purity and Danger: An Analysis of the Concepts of Pollution and Taboo*. London: Routledge, 1966.

Elinger, Karl, and Wilhelm Rudolf, eds. *Biblia Hebraica Stuttgartensia*. Stuttgart: Deutsche Bibelgesellschaft, 1998.

Gericke, Jaco. *The Hebrew Bible and Philosophy of Religion*. Atlanta: SBL, 2013.

Gunton, Colin. "Knowledge and Culture: Towards an Epistemology of the Concrete." In *The Gospel and Contemporary Culture*, edited by Hugh Montefiore, 84–102. London: Mowbray, 1992.

———. "The Truth of Christology." In *Belief in Science and in Christian Life: The Relevance of Michael Polanyi's Thought for Christian Faith and Life*, edited by T. F. Torrance, 91–107. Edinburgh: Handsel, 1980.

Hart, Trevor. *Faith Thinking: The Dynamics of Christian Theology*. Reprint, Eugene, OR: Wipf & Stock, 2005.

Hawke, Ethan, and Patricia Arquette. Interview by Terry Gross. "The Magic of the 'Boyhood' Experiment: Time and Patience." *Fresh Air*, January 13, 2015. http://www.npr.org/2015/01/13/376746926/the-magic-of-the-boyhood-experiment-time-and-patience.

Hazony, Yoram. *The Philosophy of Hebrew Scripture*. New York: Cambridge University Press, 2012.

Healy, Mary, and Robin Parry, eds. *The Bible and Epistemology: Biblical Soundings on the Knowledge of God*. Colorado Springs: Paternoster, 2007.

Hempel, Carl Gustav. "Studies in the Logic of Confirmation (I.)." *Mind*, n.s., 54.213 (1945) 1–26.

Johnson, Andrew M. "Error and Epistemological Process in the Pentateuch and Mark's Gospel: A Biblical Theology of Knowing from Foundational Texts." PhD diss., University of St Andrews, 2011.

Johnson, Dru. *Biblical Knowing: A Scriptural Epistemology of Error*. Eugene, OR: Cascade, 2013.

———. "A Biblical Nota Bene on Philosophical Inquiry." *Evangelical Theological Society* (blog). 2014. http://www.epsociety.org/library/articles.asp?pid=238.

———. *Epistemology and Biblical Theology: From the Pentateuch to the Gospel of Mark*. New York: Routledge, forthcoming.

———. *Knowledge by Ritual: A Biblical Prolegomenon to Sacramental Theology*. Journal of Theological Interpretation Supplement Series. Winona Lake, IN: Eisenbrauns, forthcoming.

Johnson, Mark S. *The Body in the Mind: The Bodily Basis of Meaning, Imagination, and Reason*. Chicago: University of Chicago Press, 1987.

Kelber, Werner H. *The Kingdom in Mark: A New Place and a New Time*. Minneapolis: Fortress, 1974.

Klawans, Jonathan. *Purity, Sacrifice, and the Temple: Symbolism and Supersessionism in the Study of Ancient Judaism*. New York: Oxford University Press, 2006.

Kline, Meredith. *By Oath Consigned: A Reinterpretation of the Covenant Signs of Circumcision and Baptism*. Grand Rapids: Eerdmans, 1975.

Kuhn, Thomas S. *The Structure of Scientific Revolutions*. 50th anniversary ed. Chicago: University of Chicago Press, 2012.

Lakoff, George. *Women, Fire, and Dangerous Things: What Categories Reveal about the Mind*. Chicago: University of Chicago Press, 1989.

Lakoff, George, and Mark Johnson. *Metaphors We Live By*. Chicago: University of Chicago Press, 1980.

Lee, Harper. *To Kill a Mockingbird*. 1st Perennial Classics ed. New York: HarperCollins, 2002.

Marcus, Joel. *Mark 8–16*. Anchor Yale Bible Commentaries. London: Yale University Press, 2009.

———. *The Way of the Lord: Christological Exegesis of the Old Testament in the Gospel of Mark*. 1st ed. Louisville: Westminster John Knox, 1992.

Meek, Esther L. *A Little Manual for Knowing*. Eugene, OR: Cascade, 2014.

———. *Longing to Know: The Philosophy of Knowledge for Ordinary People*. Grand Rapids: Brazos, 2003.

———. *Loving to Know: Covenant Epistemology*. Eugene, OR: Cascade, 2011.

Menken, Maarten J. J., and Steve Moyise, eds. *Deuteronomy in the New Testament: The New Testament and the Scriptures of Israel*. Library of New Testament Studies 358. London: T. & T. Clark, 2007.

Mgmoscatello (Wikimedia user). *Apple picture*. Image. Mar 10, 2013. http://commons.wikimedia.org/wiki/File:Apple_picture.jpg.

Moberly, R. W. L. "Did the Serpent Get It Right?" *Journal of Theological Studies* 39.1 (1988) 1–27.

———. *The Theology of the Book of Genesis*. New York: Cambridge University Press, 2009.

Moser, Paul K. *The Elusive God: Reorienting Religious Epistemology*. New York: Cambridge University Press, 2009.

Nestle, Eberhard, and Kurt Aland, eds. *Novum Testamentum Graece*. 28th ed. Stuttgart: Deutsche Bibelstiftung, 2012.

Nietzsche, Friedrich Wilhelm. *Thus Spoke Zarathustra*. Edited and translated by Walter Kaufmann. New York: Penguin, 1976.

Bibliography

————. *Twilight of the Idols: Or, How to Philosophize with a Hammer.* Translated by Richard Polt. Indianapolis: Hackett Publishing, 1997.

O'Dowd, Ryan. *The Wisdom of Torah: Epistemology in Deuteronomy and the Wisdom Literature.* Göttingen: Vandenhoeck & Ruprecht, 2009.

Plantinga, Alvin. *Warranted Christian Belief.* New York: Oxford University Press, 2000.

Polanyi, Michael. *Personal Knowledge: Towards a Post-critical Philosophy.* Chicago: University of Chicago Press, 1962.

Polkinghorne, John. *Theology in the Context of Science.* London: SPCK, 2008.

Popper, Karl R. *The Logic of Scientific Discovery.* London: Routledge, 2002.

Rad, Gerhard von. *Genesis: A Commentary.* Louisville: Westminster John Knox, 1972.

Science Council. "What Is Science?" 2015. http://www.sciencecouncil. org/definition. Scott, Ian W. *Paul's Way of Knowing: Story, Experience, and the Spirit.* Grand Rapids: Baker Academic, 2008.

Smith, James K. A. *Imagining the Kingdom: How Worship Works.* Grand Rapids: Baker Academic, 2013.

Stump, Eleonore. *Wandering in Darkness: Narrative and the Problem of Suffering.* New York: Oxford University Press, 2012.

Torrance, T. F. *Theology and Scientific Culture.* Theological Lectures at the Queen's University. Belfast: Christian Journals, 1980.

Trible, Phyllis. *God and the Rhetoric of Sexuality.* Minneapolis: Fortress, 1986.

Walker, Andrew G., and Robin A. Parry. *Deep Church Rising: The Third Schism and the Recovery of Christian Orthodoxy.* Eugene, OR: Cascade, 2014.

Wenham, Gordon. *Genesis 1–15.* Word Biblical Commentary 1. Nashville: Nelson, 1987.

Made in the USA
Middletown, DE
26 June 2020